Evangelism *as* Storytelling

EVANGELISM *as* STORYTELLING

A Reconstruction of Evangelism from a Feminist
Postcolonial Missiological Perspective

OINIKE NATALIA HAREFA

Foreword by Septemmy E. Lakawa

WIPF & STOCK · Eugene, Oregon

EVANGELISM AS STORYTELLING
A Reconstruction of Evangelism from a Feminist Postcolonial Missiological Perspective

Copyright © 2024 Oinike Natalia Harefa. All rights reserved. Except for brief quotations in critical publications or reviews, no part of this book may be reproduced in any manner without prior written permission from the publisher. Write: Permissions, Wipf and Stock Publishers, 199 W. 8th Ave., Suite 3, Eugene, OR 97401.

Wipf & Stock
An Imprint of Wipf and Stock Publishers
199 W. 8th Ave., Suite 3
Eugene, OR 97401

www.wipfandstock.com

PAPERBACK ISBN: 979-8-3852-2125-7
HARDCOVER ISBN: 979-8-3852-2126-4
EBOOK ISBN: 979-8-3852-2127-1

VERSION NUMBER 060324

Scripture quotations are taken from the New Revised Standard Version, copyright @ 1989, Division of Christian Education of the National Council of the Churches of Christ in the United States in the United States of America. Used by permission. All rights reserved.

Contents

Foreword by Septemmy E. Lakawa | vii
Preface | vii

1 INTRODUCTION | 1
  Limitations | 5
  Significance | 6
  Methodology | 6
  Structure | 7

2 THEOLOGICAL UNDERSTANDING OF EVANGELISM | 8
  Evangelism: Strategy or Lifestyle | 8
  Evangelism Explosion | 15
  Conclusion | 38

3 EVANGELISM AS MISSION FROM A POSTCOLONIAL FEMINIST MISSIOLOGICAL PERSPECTIVE | 40
  Theories of Women's Mission | 40
  Nias Cultural Patriarchalism and the Marginalization of Women's Narratives in Evangelism as Mission | 51
  Colonialism in the Traces of Evangelism as Mission | 55
  The Need to Rethink Evangelism | 60
  Conclusion | 66

4 POSTCOLONIAL RECONSTRUCTION OF EVANGELISM | 68
  Matthew 28:19–20 as a Postcolonial Narrative | 71
  Trinitarian Community as a Model of Postcolonial Missionary Community | 78
  Martyrdom as Friendship: A Form of Christian Virtue | 89
  Conclusion | 98

5 A RECONSTRUCTION OF EVANGELISM FROM A POSTCOLONIAL FEMINIST MISSIOLOGICAL PERSPECTIVE | 100
  Story Theology as Embodied Story with Prism Reading | 100
  Biography as Theology, Evangelism as Embodied Story | 104
  Hanna Blindow: The Testimony of a Woman Martyr in Nias | 110
  Dorothea Richter: The Testimony of a Friendship Opener | 124
  Sonia Parera-Hummel: The Missionary's Wife is a Missionary | 131
  Masrial Zebua: A First Woman Missionary from Nias to the Philippines | 134
  Destalenta Zega: Nias Woman Missionary at Worldwide Evangelization for Christ (WEC) | 136
  Yani Saoiyagö: Internal Missionary for the Niasan People | 139
  Postcolonial Feminist Missiological Meaning of Missionary Women's Stories | 141
  Conclusion | 145

Bibliography | 147

Foreword

Septemmy E. Lakawa

OINIKE HAREFA IS AN alumna of Sekolah Tinggi Filsafat Theologi Jakarta (Jakarta Theological Seminary). Her work is a testament to the vital intersection of mission studies, gender analysis, and feminist postcolonial theology. It is a fresh effort in these fields, offering a unique model and perspective on evangelism as storytelling. Furthermore, by linking the stories of European women missionaries and Nias women missionaries in Indonesia, the book extends the discussion on the interconnectedness of the stories of women in mission regardless of cultural, national, or geographical boundaries.

Employing Dana L. Robert's pioneering study on the thought and practice of American women in mission to analyze the narratives of European and Indonesian women missionaries, Harefa takes a critical view not only of the women's gender-based roles but also of traditional mission discourse. Her argument is constructed by and emerges from the women missionaries' brilliant, inspirational, and contextual thinking and practice.

Harefa's work challenges the conventional depiction of evangelism as a discourse and practice confined to Christian expansion. Instead, she presents a more nuanced and comprehensive view of evangelism that is intercultural, ecumenical, feminist, and postcolonial. She offers a storytelling practice that describes the encounters of women missionaries through their stories. Using the Nias culture of storytelling as a lens, her book offers a profound perspective on the importance of local cultural practices in sharing the story of the gospel. In this way, evangelism as storytelling uncovers the intricate and rich intersections of testifying, listening, telling, embodying, and witnessing to the story of Jesus Christ, drawing from the history, memory, and narratives of women, local communities, churches, and the broader communities of faith.

Harefa's book contributes to the limited research on women in mission by feminist mission theologians and to the global discourse on mission and evangelism from a feminist postcolonial theological perspective. Her book also shares the voices of Indonesian theologians with readers worldwide.

I am honored to be part of Oinike Harefa's critical project that has resulted in her first book for an Indonesian and a global readership. As her former doctoral advisor, I congratulate her, with great pride, on the publication of this book.

Preface

PROBLEMS OF PATRIARCHY AND colonialism that have left traces in the history of evangelism and Christian mission have contributed to perpetuating marginalization and discrimination against women in church life. The result is that women's narratives, in particular the narratives of women missionaries, receive less recognition and appreciation by the church. There is a need to reconstruct the concept of evangelism that is understood as a "sharing gift" and not as an instrument to dominate or subdue others, including women.

This book offers a concept of evangelism that acknowledges and respects women's roles and thoughts. I use the historical-narrative-constructive missiological method by utilizing several theories simultaneously to show the complexity of missionary women's narratives, the marginalization of their narratives, and constructive missiological efforts to reclaim their narratives as a model of embodied evangelism. These theories are the social mission theory of women in the nineteenth and twentieth centuries, postcolonial feminist mission theory, martyrdom theology, the biblical-reconstructive approach, and narrative theology.

In the end, I offer the idea of "evangelism as storytelling," namely witnessing the Trinity God through embodied storytelling of the gospel, which encourages the rediscovery of witness narratives in the form of testimonials that contain the voices, roles, experiences, and understandings of women in witnessing to the gospel. This embodied gospel is based on the incarnation of Jesus, which shows the side of God who became human in real everyday life and who leads us towards *metanoia*.

Oinike Natalia Harefa

1

INTRODUCTION

EVANGELISM IS A SIGNIFICANT part of missions. David J. Bosch discusses that if mission includes all of God's work in the world, then evangelism is the mission dimension and activity that testifies to God's work in the past, present, and future. For Bosch, evangelism and mission cannot be separated from the mission of the church.[1] Stephen B. Bevans and Roger P. Schroeder argue that being a church is being on a mission. It means being responsive to the needs of the good news in a specific context that continually requires new approaches to new situations, new societies, new cultures, and new questions as they arise.[2] Evangelism is a complex and dynamic process in which the church is enabled only by divine power to proclaim the good news to transform individuals and communities.[3]

---

1. Bosch, *Transforming Mission*, 412.
2. Bevans and Schroeder, *Constants in Context*, 31.
3. Bevans and Schroeder, *Constants in Context*, 8.

Evangelism as a mission activity is often stereotyped as Christianization. This stereotype is generally not negated by the understanding that evangelism is impossible without Christianization. If evangelism is understood as Christianization, then the meaning of evangelism is reduced to being an instrument or strategy for the church to conquer and convert those with different beliefs and cultures. This problem becomes more complicated when churches and Christian communities are in the midst of a multicultural nation like Indonesia.

Evangelism receives criticism from Dana L. Robert. According to Robert, there is significant ambiguity in evangelical and mission narratives about women's missionary work in the twentieth century and beyond.[4] This ambiguity is seen, for example, in several mission theories. By 1830, "the Christian home" theory had become the basis for sending women, specifically missionary wives, into mission work to serve as role models for other Christian families. This theory promotes ideas that value partnership between men and women in witnessing Christ in the family. However, in a hierarchical, conservative, and patriarchal cultural context, the Christian home theory limits the contribution of women (wives) to domestic roles. This ambiguity is also confirmed by the theory of "woman's works for woman," which emerged at the beginning of the twentieth century, notably in the Presbyterian U.S.A.'s missionary journal *Woman's Work for Woman*, whose first issue appeared in 1871.[5] On the one hand, this theory encourages women's involvement in missions but still in the spirit of gender complementary (not gender equality). On the other hand, gender segregation causes women's work in evangelizing to be limited to fellow women and children. According to Robert, the involvement of women missionaries increased after the establishment of schools, hospitals, orphanages, and mission stations.[6]

Missionaries are the visionaries of modern history. They generally traveled by writing notes about their thoughts and activities, which attracted historians to research the missionaries' archives. However, since 1996, public opinion about missionaries has changed. For some, missionaries are heroic figures who risked their lives for what they believed in. Later, for many historians of the late twentieth century, the missionary was seen as an ideologue, namely someone who pursued a single goal and had close relations with dominating forces such as colonialism, imperialism,

---

4. Robert, *Gospel Bearers*, xi.
5. Heuser, "*Woman's Work for Woman*."
6. Robert, "What Happened to Christian Home."

INTRODUCTION

modernization, or globalization. As a result, the understanding of missionaries becomes very narrow because they are judged based only on the goals of their mission and their relationship with power. According to Robert, the real stories and experiences of missionaries in specific locations and their encounters with the local people tend to be unnoticed in mission history.[7] In these encounters, both missionaries and local communities were challenged to experience transformation. It forms a new vision for the missionaries. Based on their vision and ministry, the understanding of who a missionary is cannot be limited by a person's gender, social class, or nationality. Missionaries are those who have a vision that is embodied by sharing their lives as a testimony to the Trinity of God to inspire conversion, liberation, justice, and transformation.

Patriarchal culture is still a major problem in world society. It causes bias in understanding who missionaries are and their roles. Patriarchy places men as the main power holders and decision-makers in the public and domestic spheres, while women play the role of servants. Patriarchy in a community becomes stronger when it meets church traditions that are also patriarchal. In a strong patriarchal church, women do not have the opportunity and power to testify the good news.

Besides the problem of patriarchy, Letty M. Russell believes that evangelism and missions in the past were the main components of cultural domination and colonialism practiced by Western missionaries in the nineteenth century and beyond. According to Russell, since the nineteenth century, missions have been understood as attempts to "implant" the Western church and culture into local communities.[8] Therefore, evangelism and missions in the history of Christianity were distorted into instruments of colonialism.

Septemmy E. Lakawa views evangelization in Indonesia, in general, as in tension between two positions: evangelization as conversion (which implies the desire to dominate other religions) and evangelization as a form of social transformation (which embraces practices against the power of domination).[9] These two dimensions are paradoxically present in evangelistic discourse in Indonesia.

In this book, I use the specific context of one of the churches in Nias Islands, namely Banua Niha Keriso Prostestan (BNKP), to show how and

---

7. Robert, *Converting Colonialism*, 1.
8. Russell, "Cultural Hermeneutics," 24.
9. Lakawa, "Mission and Evangelism."

why evangelism today needs to consider the feminist postcolonial missiological perspective in mission. BNKP is one of the churches that existed in Indonesia because of the missionary work sent by the Rheinische Missionsgesellschaft (RMG) in Germany. In the history of the mission, women missionaries from Germany have inspired the Niasan women to get an education. However, there has been no fair recognition and appreciation for women missionaries. Women's narratives, experiences, and understanding of evangelism and missions have not been included in the history of the church and missions in Nias.

Since the history of mission and evangelism contains traces of patriarchy and colonialism, there is a need for churches to construct their understanding of mission and evangelism. The problems of patriarchy and colonialism, which have left traces in the history of Christian evangelization and missions, have helped perpetuate marginalization and discrimination against women in the church. The result is that women's narratives, especially woman missionary narratives, receive less recognition and appreciation from the church.

There is a need to construct a concept of evangelism that is understood as "sharing gifts" and not as an instrument to dominate others, including women and local culture. Authentic evangelism is contrary to the goals and ideas of patriarchal and colonial domination. Currently, Christianity needs an evangelism concept that learns from historical failures in the past. Evangelism is expected to be able to answer today's challenges to achieve liberation, justice, and equality, especially for women. The church needs an evangelism concept that provides greater space for women and local traditions to have their voices heard.

I offer the idea of evangelism as storytelling, namely witnessing the Trinitarian God through the embodied story of the gospel testimony. The gospel as embodied story is based on the incarnation of Jesus, which shows the God who became human in real everyday life. God's incarnation (embodiment) aims to enable humans to enter into a Trinitarian relationship. This entrance was made possible through the incarnation of the Word that became a body. Jesus said, "This is My body . . . this is My blood" (Matt 26:26–28). Jesus as Word is a metaphor for the embodied story. The story of Christ was made flesh in bread and wine. So, people who receive this symbol are involved in the metaphor of the body because the symbol of body and blood has become a presence in the lives of people both collectively and individually. In the concept of evangelism, the gospel as embodied story is manifested in testimonies, namely the stories of women whose belief in the Trinitarian God has brought hope for survival, and freedom from oppression, strengthened solidarity, and encouraged transformation specifically for fellow women.

The gospel as an embodied story is manifested in the narrative of martyrdom, namely the Christian presence through the voices, roles, experiences, and understanding of women who are specific and significant in evangelization. The story that forms it is a testimony of giving and sharing life through fair and equal friendly relations in cross-border spaces, especially for voices that have been marginalized, to participate in the invitation to *missio Dei*. The Trinitarian God who is in a just and equal relationship also invites humans to witness love for others who are different without being limited by nationality, race, class, sex, and gender.

Storytelling touches on the dimensions of witnessing, sharing, and acting. In a story, there is teaching, surprise, flexibility, and acceptance. In Nias society, the term "storytelling" is known as *famanö-manö*. Through *manö-manö* (stories), storytellers pass on moral values and virtues of life to their listeners. There is power in storytelling and that power is not intended to dominate (power over), but to be shared (power with); that power does not take the form of coercion, but an invitation to act. Storytelling as evangelism has the power to influence, even invite, other people who are in similar situations or struggle to find patterns of "conversion" that help them answer life's struggles. When a group of people hear the stories of others' struggles, they have the opportunity to broaden their perspectives beyond their own subjective experience of viewing the world.[10] Conversion is *metanoia*, a changing habits, priorities, and life goals to obtain salvation, healing, liberation, and transformation.[11] Telling the stories of women's lives in mission work is a form of evangelism because their life journeys are a testimony to the Triune God in the world. By telling women's life stories, their voices become significant and can contribute to a new understanding of evangelism.

LIMITATIONS

I limit the scope of this book to several parts. First, this book focuses on the study of evangelism as storytelling based on a postcolonial feminist missiological perspective at BNKP. The document that is specifically elaborated is

10. Love, "John Henry Newman's *Apologia*."
11. WCC, *Together towards Life*.

the *Evangelism Explosion* (*EE*) for adults,[12] which is analyzed through the lens of the church's ecumenical document, namely *Together towards Life: Mission and Evangelism in Changing Landscapes* (*TTL*). Second, it focuses on exploring and analyzing several theories of women's mission, namely the Christian home, woman's work for woman, world friendship, and partnership. Third, this book discusses the need for postcolonial reconstruction of evangelism, namely the narrative of the Gospel of Matthew as a narrative of marginalized communities, the concept of the Trinity as a model of postcolonial mission communities, and the concept of martyrdom as a form of Christian virtue. In the end, this book focuses on the stories of female missionaries. There are three categories of female missionaries in this study: women from Germany who have been sent by RMG and have come to the Nias Islands, Indonesian women missionaries sent by RMG but non-Nias (hybrid), and local women missionaries from Nias.

SIGNIFICANCE

This book constructs a model of contemporary evangelism that is useful for theological discourse, especially in the discipline of missiology and postcolonial feminism. It challenges the theology of church mission from a postcolonial feminist missiological perspective. For churches, this book raises an understanding of evangelism from women's voices, which encourages transformation in evangelism in the church. Specifically for the churches in Asia, this study is important to strengthen the theology of evangelism and mission. For church members, this book offers a different perspective that enriches the horizons of evangelism and mission. It also provides benefits to mission organizations around the world to develop an evangelism model that is relevant and contextual today. This book is specifically useful for theological colleges and churches in Indonesia and also the United Evangelical Mission (UEM), an institution that previously sent missionaries to Nias, in developing an evangelism model that is relevant and contextual today.

METHODOLOGY

This book used a historical-narrative-constructive missiological method by utilizing several theories simultaneously to show the complexity of

---

12. Kennedy, *Multiplikasi*.

INTRODUCTION

women's missionary narratives, the marginalization of their narratives, and constructive missiological efforts to reclaim their narratives as models of embodied evangelism. These theories are the social theory of North American women's mission in the nineteenth and twentieth centuries, postcolonial feminist mission theory, martyrdom theology, the biblical-reconstructive approach to Matt 28:18–20, and narrative theology. This theoretical perspective is used to collect, analyze, and interpret data. The data in this research consists of written data, namely personal journals (unpublished) and publications of female missionaries available in the Archiv und Museum Stiftung der VEM, the WCC documents *TTL*, EE documents for adults, and mission and church history books at BNKP. Apart from that, oral data was collected through interviews with several local women missionaries at BNKP.

STRUCTURE

This book consists of five chapters. Chapter 1 is the introduction, which consists of the background of the problem, problem formulation, limitations, methodology, and structure of the book. Chapter 2 discusses the church's theological views on evangelism. The document specifically examined is the *EE* for adults. This document is analyzed based on the *TTL* document. Chapter 3 is about evangelism as a mission from a postcolonial feminist missiological perspective. This chapter contains theories of women's mission, an analysis of patriarchal culture, and the influence of colonialism on evangelism in the church, as well as the need to rethink evangelism. Chapter 4 is a postcolonial reconstruction of evangelism. This reconstruction focuses on three specific parts, namely the biblical narrative of evangelism in the Gospel of Matthew, the concept of the Trinitarian God as a model for postcolonial mission communities, and martyrdom as friendship. Chapter 5 is my theological construction, namely evangelism as storytelling. In this section, the stories of female missionaries from RMG and BNKP are presented as embodied gospel narratives, namely women's testimonies and also life experiences as testimonies of the Trinitarian God and God's work. These stories are raised as theological sources for evangelization that is just, liberating, and transformational.

2

THEOLOGICAL UNDERSTANDING OF EVANGELISM

EVANGELISM: STRATEGY OR LIFESTYLE

EVANGELISM IS ROOTED IN the Greek word *euangelion*, which means gospel. Bosch used the term *evangelism* to refer to activities that include the preaching of the gospel and theological reflection on these activities.[1] He provides some insight into evangelism. For him, evangelism is a mission, but a mission is broader than evangelism. Evangelism is an essential dimension of all church activity that includes witnessing what God has done, is doing, and will do. The goal of evangelism is to get a response, namely conversion or life transformation. This response is not coercive but always an invitation. Therefore, the preacher of the gospel is as a witness and not as a judge. As a testimony, evangelism is possible only by a community of believers. The testimony is a manifestation of Christian faith followed by a lifestyle. Evangelism offers salvation as a "gift," so its goals cannot be equated with proselytism, church expansion, or member recruitment. Authentic evangelism is always contextual. Evangelism cannot be separated from preaching and actions to struggle for justice.[2]

According to Bevans and Schroeder, evangelism has two forms, namely witness and proclamation.[3] Evangelism as a witness means "a way of life"

---

1. Bosch, *Transforming Mission*, 409.
2. Bosch, *Transforming Mission*, 411–19.
3. Bevans and Schroeder, *Constants in Context*, 352.

(lifestyle) that shows the authenticity of Christian life, while evangelism as a proclamation is the foundation, peak, and center of the gospel. These two forms of evangelism demonstrate the mission of Jesus Christ through "words and actions." As a witness, evangelism means the words and actions of a person or Christian community that confirm a statement of faith in Jesus Christ. Evangelism is an invitation for others to respond. Thus, the witness contains a proclamation. The witness referred to by Bevans and Schroeder is a lifestyle and existence that testify to Christ.

Evangelism as a witness can take the form of individual, local Christian community, institutional, and common witness of a larger community.[4] Evangelism as an individual witness is the lifestyle of a person who lives in the light of faith. It includes missionaries who, despite all their limitations as humans, still live in simplicity and view Christ as their life model. Every believer is also called to be a witness with integrity, an intimate life with the divine, manifested in daily life through faith, love, and hope. Evangelism as a community witness refers to the life of the local community who have encountered and enlivened the gospel. This community does not live for itself but in solidarity with others through love. Evangelism as an institutional witness shows that the essence of a witness is institutional. The church is more than just a local community; the essence of the church is universal. The church becomes a community that moves outside itself and grows in an environment that becomes schools, hospitals, orphanages, and various other institutions that also witness to God, so giving life becomes a culture of these institutions. Evangelism as a common witness is when various Christian traditions from diverse backgrounds work together to witness to God through joint prayer, cooperation for justice, offering countercultural testimony, helping others, participating in education, theological research, and so on.[5]

Evangelism as proclamation is communicating the gospel, the mystery of salvation revealed by God in Jesus Christ with the power of the Holy Spirit. Bevans and Schroeder wrote down several characters of the proclamation.[6] First, proclamation is the activity of communicating the gospel about the entire story of the life of Jesus Christ, starting from his ministry, death, and resurrection. The entire narrative holistically takes and introduces humans to the transcendent God. Second, proclamations are

---

4. Bevans and Schroeder, *Constants in Context*, 353.
5. Bevans and Schroeder, *Constants in Context*, 353.
6. Bevans and Schroeder, *Constants in Context*, 358–360.

always invitations and never coercive. Therefore, proselytism is not a form of evangelism. Third, proclamation provides answers to questions, especially giving reasons for hope and also stating the truth. For this reason, listening is also part of the proclamation. Fourth, proclamation is an activity with humility so that it is in contrast to a superior position over others or like a giver to a recipient. Proclamation is not colonization or exploitation of others but rather communicates the gospel to all people with humility as a sign of God's reign that reveals grace, love, and justice in the world.

Robert also understands evangelism as testimony but with a different emphasis than Bosch, Bevans, and Schroeder. She pays special attention to how women are involved in evangelism as "gospel bearers" amid "gender barriers."[7] Early women missionaries did not have as many opportunities for evangelization as male missionaries had. However, women missionaries found different forms of evangelism so that they could be actively involved in evangelism and missions. For instance, evangelism is conducted not only as conveying the gospel verbally but also as an opportunity to build relationships in liminal spaces.

In Robert's analysis of mission history, evangelism for women missionaries was connected to hospitality.[8] Although women missionaries were interested in spreading the gospel, social customs and church regulations usually prevented them from becoming missionaries. Evangelism and mission activities were usually considered men's duties. In such circumstances, hospitality becomes a form of evangelism used by women to get involved in evangelism. Hospitality begins at home, namely when visits and conversations occur. Visiting non-Christian women in their homes became the main means and opportunity for women missionaries to witness to the gospel.

The roots of hospitality as evangelism lie in the New Testament when Jesus urged his followers to welcome strangers. Throughout Christian history, hospitality was a very important context for women missionaries in situations where preaching the gospel in the public sphere was difficult or even impossible due to cultural barriers that prohibited women from leading public activities. Hospitality often encourages the opening up of liminal spaces between the completely public and the very private. This space is where someone is invited and cared for. Hospitality to strangers in need is a mission of inclusion. Missionary women have typically situated

---

7. Robert, *Gospel Bearers*.
8. Robert, *Christian Mission*, 138.

cross-cultural transmission of the gospel within a framework of service, healing, teaching, and hospitality. They are remembered as sisters, mothers, teachers, social workers, evangelists, or medical doctors, whose witness to the gospel helped build relationships. Even when conversion was impossible, the network of relations between women had been the primary means by which Christian ideas and values crossed cultural boundaries.

In the context of Southeast Asia, Lakawa formulates a mission as a call to "witness together" the truth and light of the Living God amid Asian reality today.[9] The mission is border crossing, multidimensional, and multidirectional. According to Lakawa, evangelism in Southeast Asia has always been in the paradox of mission history between evangelism as "conversion" with a sense of religious domination and also "social transformation" that challenges domination.

The view of evangelism understood by Bosch, Bevans and Schroeder, Robert, and Lakawa shows that evangelism is a lifestyle of witnessing. Bosch emphasizes evangelism as the message of the gospel, which leads to the transformation of lives. Bevans and Schroeder understand evangelism as testimony and proclamation, namely a way of living to witness to Christ through words and deeds. Robert emphasizes the roles of women in evangelism in liminal spaces, namely hospitality as a style of women missionaries. Meanwhile, Lakawa sees the paradox of evangelism in Southeast Asia, which is between the two, namely evangelism as conversion and evangelism as social transformation.

The history of evangelism and missions in Nias is different than the views of previous scholars in the theology of evangelism. In the Nias context, Uwe Hummel and Tuhoni Telaumbanua in *Cross and Adu* show how missionaries in the past clearly understood evangelism "as a strategy" to convert local people from tribal religion to Christianity. Ludwig E. Denninger reports that from his arrival in 1865 until 1869, not a single Niasan had become a Christian because their belief in *Adu* was still very strong. Other early missionaries such as Wilhelm Ködding and August Mohring used strategies to convert the people of Nias to Christianity by distributing gifts such as money, tobacco, or clothing. However, this strategy was less successful. These missionaries realized that the Nias people came to religious services only to get these gifts.[10]

---

9. Lakawa, "Mission and Evangelism."
10. Hummel and Telaumbanua, *Cross and Adu*, 107.

Evangelism as a strategy can also be seen from the approach used by the early missionaries in Nias who built strong relationships with local authorities, namely the *salawa* (village elders) and the Dutch East Indies government. In 1873, an RMG missionary, Wilhelm Thomas, finally succeeded in baptizing four people in the Ombölata area. The key to his success was the support of local authorities. Thomas built close relations with the Dutch East Indies government so that his position was quite respected in the eyes of the people of Nias. This power relations approach was also used by the director of RMG, Lothar Schreiner, who collaborated with the Dutch East Indies government at that time. Since 1901, the Dutch East Indies government supported the RMG mission in Nias as long as it was in line with their "ethical politics."[11]

Before the presence of the RMG, the Vereenigde Osstindische Compagnie (VOC) had existed in Nias since 1660.[12] To control trade in Nias, the VOC used military force and strategic approaches with local authorities, namely *salawa* or *si'ulu*, so that the Nias people would sell their products to the VOC. Local leaders also benefited from the taxation of trade proceeds. Production in the form of agriculture was limited in Nias, so in 1693–1740, the VOC with the cooperation of *salawa* and *si'ulu* exchanged gold with slaves from Nias.[13] Since 1824, the Dutch East Indies government had administrative power in Nias. The presence of the Dutch East Indies government was not taken for granted by the people of Nias, especially in southern Nias and central Nias. People's rebellions occurred in several places, for example in the Ma'u area. In 1903, the Dutch East Indies government issued a new regulation that the Nias people would no longer be controlled by *salawa* and *si'ulu* but by the Dutch East Indies government. Since then, forced labor (*rodi*) for the construction of roads and bridges was implemented. Likewise, the people of Nias were required to move their settlements from the highlands to the lowlands, and they were forced to plant crops that benefited the Dutch East Indies government such as coconuts and rice.[14]

Based on this history, a postcolonial reading shows that there were layers of power in Nias society, namely the power of the Dutch East Indies government and also the power of traditional Nias leaders. The relations

---

11. Hummel and Telaumbanua, *Cross and Adu*, 274.
12. Hummel and Telaumbanua, *Salib dan Adu*, 61.
13. Hummel and Telaumbanua, *Salib dan Adu*, 61.
14. Hummel and Telaumbanua, *Salib dan Adu*, 66.

that occur between existing powers are not always mutually antagonistic. Sometimes transactional relations occurred between the rulers of the Dutch East Indies and the local leaders of Nias.

When RMG came to Nias, this pattern of power relations was also visible. On the one hand, cooperation with the Dutch East Indies government benefited the RMG missionaries because they were given space to carry out their missions. The missionaries benefited because the Nias people who were conquered by the Dutch East Indies government finally converted to Christianity. On the other hand, the missionaries were also made to submit to the authority of the Dutch East Indies government. They could not speak out and did nothing when the Nias people were colonized and required to do forced labor by the Dutch East Indies government. Likewise, when the Dutch conquered villages in Nias by first conquering local leaders, the missionaries did not defend them.

Around 1915–1930, evangelization in Nias encouraged *Fangesa Dödö* (the Great Awakening).[15] Apart from evangelization efforts, this mass conversion was also influenced by social changes, such as the identity crisis that occurred within the people of Nias. This crisis is increasingly felt by the lack of influence of local leaders, customs, and religion of the Nias ethnic.

This mass conversion movement was responded to by the missionaries with a personal approach strategy. The missionaries did not perform mass baptisms but chose to emphasize personal evangelism. Evangelism leads a person to personal conversion from their local belief. The conversion includes maintaining the purity of life from all talismans, magic, and symbols of local beliefs. To ensure that the Nias people who had converted to Christianity maintained the purity of their lives, church discipline was formulated, namely the rules that a Christian must obey.

From 1930 to 1965, missionaries focused on preventing the people of Nias from returning to their local beliefs. Since then, the emphasis on evangelism began to be connected to social transformation, specifically through Christian education with catechism teaching.[16] At this time, the people of Nias who chose to embrace Christianity felt the benefits of education, health, and security facilities from the missionaries.

Since evangelism was connected to social transformation, women missionaries began to be significant because they were sent by mission institutions to educate local communities, especially women and children.

---

15. Hummel and Telaumbanua, *Salib dan Adu*, 284.
16. Hummel and Telaumbanua, *Salib dan Adu*, 285.

Women missionaries from the RMG, such as Hanna Blindow, Dorothea Richter, and Sonia Parera-Hummel are examples of figures from the RMG who went to Nias. They brought a change in view that evangelism was no longer narrowly understood as a Christianization strategy but as a unique lifestyle of witnessing. The problem is that the narratives of their lives and service as missionaries in Nias have not been appreciated by the church.

Based on the mission history, at least three issues receive my criticism of past evangelism in Nias. First, the understanding of evangelism based on the history of missions in Nias still has a patriarchal character. This situation is in line with Robert's criticism that, in mission history, women's narratives are generally not included. Meanwhile, for Robert, evangelism is not only a verbal preaching of the gospel as understood by male missionaries but also an opportunity to build relationships in liminal spaces or what is called "hospitality." BNKP's understanding and practice of evangelism in the past were still centered on the understanding of male missionaries. This also can be proven in mission history books at BNKP, such as *Benih yang Tumbuh XIII*.[17]

Second, the model of evangelization in Nias in the past was influenced by the spirit of colonialism, which was manifested through how the missionaries valued and dealt with local beliefs and cultures that were considered inferior and had to be replaced with Christianity. According to Bosch, the goal of evangelism is to obtain a response, namely conversion or life transformation. This response is not obtained through manipulative or coercive means but is always an invitation. Evangelism in the spirit of colonialism is closely linked to efforts to dominate others, while authentic evangelism is a "sharing gift" and an "invitation" to live in the light of the gospel. "The gift" is not a form of money, tobacco, or clothes but rather the gift of the good news about God and God's work for humankind so that there will be a transformation towards the fullness of life in Christ Jesus. Lakawa assesses that evangelization in Southeast Asia, specifically in Indonesia, has always been in the paradox of mission history, namely between evangelization as conversion with a sense of religious domination and also social transformation that challenges this domination. This paradoxical model of evangelism can be found in later models of women's evangelism in Nias, which paid a lot of attention to education, health, and community sanitation.

Third, the understanding of evangelism in the past was still instrumental. Evangelism is understood as a strategy to recruit adherents of

---

17. Gulö, *Benih yang Tumbuh XIII*.

different beliefs to become Christians. Instrumental evangelism is very focused on the issue of strategies that are a way to achieve the expected goals. Inauthentic evangelism strategies aim at proselytism and member recruitment using various methods including manipulation and coercion. Bevans and Schroeder understand evangelism not as an instrument but as a testimony (a way to live) and as a proclamation. Meanwhile, the initial evangelization strategy in the history of missions in Nias can be classified as a form of covert proselytism aimed at converting adherents of local religious beliefs to Christianity. This proselytism was deliberately carried out by missionaries, even by giving gifts such as money, tobacco, or clothing. Giving goods with the motive to recruit members is a manipulative way to dominate others. In this way, the "giver" feels powerful over the "recipient." One of the consequences is the creation of a power relationship, namely when the recipient is subdued to follow the wishes of the giver.

The church needs to honestly and humbly admit that in history, evangelism has been distorted by strategies of evangelism that were oriented toward recruiting believers. The way of evangelism that prioritizes strategy rather than the lifestyle of witnessing is a challenge in contemporary evangelism. When evangelism is understood as a mere strategy, it is exposed to becoming a tool to manipulate and dominate others. The integration between patriarchy and colonialization results in the instrumentalization of others who are seen as inferior, including women.

EVANGELISM EXPLOSION

One of the contemporary evangelism models currently developing in Indonesia is Evangelism Explosion (EE). The EE model was initiated by D. James Kennedy. Kennedy was a pastor at Coral Ridge Presbyterian Church in America. He was born on November 3, 1930, and died on September 5, 2007. He started EE in 1962 as a ministry to train Christians to personally share their faith and lead others to Christ. In 1974, Kennedy established a vision not only for the church's mission but also for the media ministry. He spoke about his vision to his congregation and said to them, "Our prayer is that through this church, the Gospel of Jesus Christ may be broadcast through television and radio, films and cassettes, books and clinics, and in unimaginable ways throughout the world, that command Christ to go and preach the Gospel to every creature may be fulfilled in our generation."[18]

---

18. Kennedy, *Multiplikasi*, 11. See https://www.crm.tv for the continuation of Kennedy's

Kennedy developed EE models for forty years. According to him, the concepts discussed in EE are training materials for the Christian community. EE is prepared for church leaders who desire to equip their members to engage in evangelism. There are four approaches to EE, namely friendship, evangelism, discipleship, and church growth.[19] Kennedy organized EE materials in the form of a combination of lectures, demonstrations, and practice in conveying the gospel.

The EE model of evangelism has been used by churches in 212 countries, including Indonesia. EE has been present since 1984 in Indonesia. BNKP is one of the churches in Indonesia that implemented EE until today. The memorandum of agreement between BNKP and EE Indonesia has been in existence since April 5, 1993.[20] However, until today, there has been no analysis carried out by BNKP of the practice and theology of the EE model.

Church documents in BNKP such as church order and confession stated the limited understanding of mission and evangelism. In the preamble of BNKP Church Order in 2007, it is written:

> BNKP acknowledges that Jesus Christ is Lord and Savior according to the testimony of the Bible and is called to preach/witness the Kingdom of God in this world. To realize God's will on earth, the church is called to carry out God's mission, which is realized by all church members in developing and renewing the world.[21]

Chapter 2 of the BNKP Church Order, concerning the "Nature and Existence of the Church," says:

> BNKP is the church of the Lord Jesus Christ which currently exists as congregations, resorts, and synods in Indonesia, carrying out God's mission in the world.[22]

Based on the BNKP Confession in 2022, the church's mission is formulated as follows:

> BNKP believes and teaches that the church is called and sent to witness and preach the Gospel of Jesus Christ or "Good News" to

vision.

19. Kennedy, *Multiplikasi*, 11.
20. Kennedy, *Multiplikasi*, 11.
21. Majelis Sinode BNKP, *Ketetapan Majelis*, preamble.
22. Majelis Sinode BNKP, *Ketetapan Majelis*, ch. 2, art. 6, para. 1.

THEOLOGICAL UNDERSTANDING OF EVANGELISM

all creation (Mark 16:15). The church's calling must continue the mission of Jesus Christ who was sent by God to save this world and reconcile all things with God, through fellowship, testimony, and complete service. This calling task of the church applies in all places and throughout the ages contextually.

The Triune God, who called and sent the church (Matthew 28:18–20; Matthew 10:16; Luke 9:2; Acts 15:27; 22:21). Therefore, the mission of the church is the mission of God (Latin = *missio Dei*). This means that in carrying out its mission, the church is only involved in God's mission, so what the church must do is carry out God's Will; not the will and interests of the church.

BNKP believes and teaches that the church must submit to the power and will of God. A church that only pays attention to its interests is a church that fails to carry out its calling. And the church continually renews itself in realizing its calling.[23]

Based on the BNKP Church Order and Confession, there is an understanding that the church is called to witness the good news to all creation. Mission is based on belief in the Trinitarian God, and the church is called to be involved in God's mission. However, in those documents, there is no specific mention of BNKP's understanding of evangelism. Therefore, there is a need to formulate a theology of evangelism in BNKP today. To conduct mission and evangelism activity, BNKP implemented the EE model.

In this section, I focus on the analysis of EE for adults. There are two EE materials for adults that are specifically analyzed. The first material is *Multiplikasi: Evangelism Explosion International Indonesia*.[24] This is a handbook for EE trainers that contains a complete explanation of EE. The second material is a tractate entitled *Do You Know for Sure?*[25] This tractate is addressed to participants in evangelism training. The tractate is packaged in the form of a simple pocketbook that is easy for participants to follow because it is presented concisely through stories and illustrations.

EE analysis is useful for answering several questions researched to find the theological view of evangelism in BNKP. The first question is: What makes the EE model of evangelism attractive and growing in BNKP? Do EE's theological themes reflect an authentic theology of evangelism? Does EE provide a fair space for women to be involved and have their

23. BPMS BNKP, *Konfesi*, art. 10.
24. Kennedy, *Multiplikasi*.
25. Kennedy, *Apakah Anda Tahu*.

voices heard, or does it still perpetuate patriarchy and colonization, and is it instrumental? These three questions guide the analysis. To answer these questions, I direct the EE analysis into three major parts. The first part is an analysis of EE through empirical observation to find out what helped the EE model be so interesting to and accepted by the BNKP. The second part is an analysis of EE's theological views using the theological paradigm categories by Bevans and Schroeder. The third part is EE challenged by the document *Together towards Life: Mission and Evangelism in Changing Landscapes* (*TTL*). The end of this section leads to an analysis of whether EE provides a fair space for women to engage in evangelism.

Empirical Observations

This observation was carried out to observe and analyze strategies, trainer style, participant responses, teamwork, training situations, and follow-up to the EE model. The observations were made by recording events that occurred during the EE training held at the BNKP Kota Gunungsitoli church on September 12–15, 2022, for 150 participants. The participants were young people who were taking catechism classes. This training was led directly by the EE team, namely Simon and Yosephien Siahaan. The main team was assisted by a local team from Nias. Among the team members, some serve as tutors, worship leaders, multimedia officers, musicians, and local committee members.

Strategy

In the beginning, the team introduced a new edition of the EE book entitled *Share It*. This book is an EE training edition that has undergone technical modifications and adjustments with a more organized appearance so that it is easier for participants to learn. The book's content is no different than the early edition, *Multiplikasi: Evangelism Explosion International Indonesia*. *Share It* materials are prepared to equip participants with intensive training of four to five days (thirty-five to forty hours). The training time is divided into fifteen hours of meetings, which include theory, simulation, and field practice.

According to Yosephien Siahaan, the *Share It* edition was designed and published to make it easier to convey the good news sharply and effectively. The aim of the training is for participants to be able to testify about

God and carry out the Great Commission. In addition to *Share It*, there is also the tractate *Do You Know for Sure?* This tractate is in the form of a small pocketbook to facilitate participants when carrying out the practice of evangelizing others. In this training, the book and the tractate are used together.

An explanation of the EE training series is followed by an explanation of the EE training mission statement, namely: "We exist to glorify God by equipping local churches throughout the world to multiply through friendship, evangelism, discipleship, and healthy church growth."[26] There are three objectives of EE training: the participants have certainty of salvation, the participants are equipped to preach the gospel effectively to others, and the participants make witnessing a lifestyle so that multiplication happens.[27]

There are four biblical principles to *Share It* training. First, every Christian is a witness of Christ because they are the most strategic key but are often not yet empowered for world evangelization (Acts 1:8). Second, the responsibility of the pastor is to equip the saints (Eph 4:11–12). Third, the best way to equip yourself is not just with theory but with field practice. Fourth, multiplication can occur if participants not only become witnesses but are also able to train other people to become witnesses like themselves (Acts 6:7; 2 Tim 2:2).

This training began with an oral explanation of EE as a "Divine Mega Project" that is lived and carried out as a manifestation of the Great Commission of the Lord Jesus Christ. The first part of the session began with prayers, praise songs, and words of motivation that fueled the participants' enthusiasm.

After general explanations, the tutors took turns presenting a series of EE training sessions. The series of sessions began with the themes of friendship, presentation of the gospel (five main theological topics: grace, man, God, Christ, faith), self-surrender, and direct follow-up.

Trainer Style

Each session began with an introduction to the trainer who would bring the material to the session. The introduction was not monotonous but was accompanied by jokes and motivational words that encouraged the participants. When the trainer delivered the material, participants paid attention

26. Kennedy, *Multiplikasi*, 2.
27. Kennedy, *Multiplikasi*, 10.

to the trainer, who was speaking while reading the *Share It* that had been distributed. The left side of each page of *Share It* is the scheme and flow of each topic as well as a collection of questions and answers to the dialogue that occurs during evangelism. The section is also supplemented by pictorial illustrations provided in the EE tractate. The right side of each page is a complete explanation of the topics discussed.

The trainer's style is confident and enthusiastic. EE trainers have communicative skills to relate to participants and also master the material presented to participants. These materials are available in the form of PowerPoint slides and simulation videos. The trainer also speaks freely and communicates through dialogue, namely questions and answers with the participants to elicit their views on key terms on each topic discussed.

One of the sessions was delivered by a trainer named Noverlianus Harefa.[28] He started his part of the session by sharing a personal story about what blessings he had received by attending EE training. He said that he had received two blessings. The first was the certainty of safety. Second was the ability to equip others to witness the gospel.

Before starting a new session, the trainer always reminds the participants about the essence of the topics that have been studied previously so that they remember it again. This repetition also functions to connect topics that have been studied with new topics that will be studied. Apart from that, there is also the use of everyday assumptions or examples to make it easier for participants to understand the topic being discussed.

Participant Responses

Based on my observations, the participants were very enthusiastic about taking part in this training. The tutor explained for around fifteen to thirty minutes, then continued with a video demonstration. All of the demonstration videos were played by female actors. After the demonstration video was played, the activity continued with a simulation by the participants. Participants could express themselves in the simulation by imitating what had been shown in the video demonstration. This part was considered exciting by the participants because they tried to imitate the conversations they had witnessed through the simulation video. After this series of sessions was finished, the trainer again reviewed the main points of the topics discussed simply.

28. Although we have the same family name, Noverlianus Harefa is unrelated to me.

Teamwork

In this EE training, team collaboration was very good. Among the team, some serve as tutors or coaches, worship leaders, multimedia officers, and music players, and there was also a local committee that provided logistical needs and food during the training. Each team member knew their duties and roles and was responsive when other team members needed help. Team members were there not only when it was their turn to be on duty but took part in all ongoing training sessions. At the beginning and the end of the training, this special team always prayed and submitted this series of training to God's care.

Training Situation

The training situation was quite dynamic. Both trainers and participants took part in this EE training activity with great enthusiasm. Training activities did not seem boring because both trainers and participants played an active role and communicated with each other. Each session went smoothly.

Training Follow-up

Part of the follow-up training was that participants were asked to fill out a spiritual birth certificate in the tractate *Do You Know for Sure?* Participants were encouraged to experience new life in fellowship and grow in faith in God. This growth in faith can be measured by spiritual activities, namely reading the Bible, communicating with God through prayer, attending services every Sunday, attending fellowship, and also being a witness.

To be witnesses, participants were invited again to remember the five main theological topics in the EE model. To make it easier, participants were invited to remember by demonstrating the five fingers: grace on the thumb, human on the index finger, God on the middle finger, Christ on the ring finger, and faith on the little finger.

Participants were then invited to follow practical steps in evangelism. A witness's first duty is to start a conversation and build a friendship. Then, the witness turns the interlocutor's attention to spiritual topics as an initial step in evangelism. Several examples of how to start a conversation topic are also provided in several versions, including anticipation of possible answers from the interlocutor. Participants are also provided with strategies for providing feedback on possible answers. For example, "If you were asked to rate your life using the numbers one to ten, what would your life value be? Why do you judge by that number?" or "If there was God's presence in your life, would it make your life meaningful?" The interlocutor will be allowed to provide answers without interruption from the witness. When a witness has finished speaking, the witness can start giving personal testimony.

Based on this EE model, personal testimony is a story based on the witness's encounter with Christ. This story must be packaged in such a way that it is interesting and arouses the spiritual interest of the interlocutor, so that there is no rejection. Some things to pay attention to when practicing personal testimony are not using Christian terms. According to Yosephien Siahaan, this consideration was taken because we are in Indonesia, a country with plural religions and beliefs. Personal testimonies are also packaged in three stages, namely life before, during, and after accepting Jesus. A witness can use metaphorical language to refer to Jesus Christ as "a wise father" or "a friend." Likewise with the mention of the Bible, so that it is not explicitly mentioned, it can be replaced with "a book."

Other Elements

During training, there were other elements used to support the main material, including music, video simulations, and illustrative images. The types of illustrations or messages used in everyday life were stories that are contained in EE books.

Analysis Based on Empirical Observations

Based on my observations, several interesting things need to be appreciated and also criticized in the EE model. First, EE from the beginning was an evangelism strategy to multiply believers to become Christians. EE has an advantage in terms of practical strategy because this evangelism model is equipped with material that is continuously being developed, in the form of both books and videos that are specifically packaged to be easy to follow. EE materials are also interesting because they are a combination of lectures, demonstrations, and practice of conveying the gospel. This strategy is also packaged simply. Each session is followed by a simulation by the training participants so that they can easily remember what they have learned. EE materials offer practical evangelism strategies rather than comprehensive theological explanations. Therefore, EE is attractive for churches that do not yet have a practical evangelism model, for example, BNKP, because its presence answers the church's need for an evangelism model that can be directly applied in the field.

The EE strategy has four approaches, namely friendship, evangelism, discipleship, and church growth.[29] These four approaches need to be confronted with the motivation of evangelism. However, authentic evangelism is based on the character of sharing gifts and is invitational. Based on this character, the EE approach needs to be criticized. For example, the initial EE approach used the term "friendship." Friendship is used as the entrance to the gospel message, which ultimately leads to the goal of multiplication. Friendship as an entry point in EE's evangelism is very different than Robert's view. Learning from how women in the past were involved in evangelism, Robert understands evangelism as a space of hospitality in which to witness to the gospel. From a hospitality perspective, the friendship that Robert means is not a superficial form of friendship or simply an entry point for multiplication purposes. Friendship with a foundation of hospitality becomes a space of inclusion where the transmission of the gospel expands and becomes a framework for service, healing, and teaching. Even when multiplication does not occur, the network of relationships between women in friendship become the main means by which Christian ideas and values cross cultural boundaries.

Second, EE begins with a burning passion for witnessing. This is demonstrated by the EE trainers through their coaching style and compact teamwork. This enthusiasm is also transmitted to training participants. Kennedy, the figure who initiated EE from the beginning, had a vision that the gospel of Jesus Christ could be broadcast and that Christ's command to go and preach the gospel to every creature would be fulfilled in the current generation. After more than 157 years of the gospel arriving on Nias Island in 1865, there is a desire for BNKP to have a burning spirit of evangelism. This enthusiasm recalls memories of the past about missionaries who also came to bring the gospel to Nias. This memory is refreshed every time the annual celebration of the Coming of the Gospel Day in Nias on September 27.

Passion in evangelism is important, but vigilance is needed so that evangelism does not shift into a passion for dominating others. Kennedy's

---

29. Kennedy, *Multiplikasi*, 11.

vision that the mission of the church be fulfilled in this generation shows that in the EE model, there is a high orientation towards the number of evangelists and towards multiplying the number of people who become Christians. Kennedy's vision is very different than Bosch's view of evangelism. For Bosch, evangelism offers salvation as a gift, so its aims cannot be equated with proselytism, church expansion, or member recruitment.

Third, EE training has a pedagogical element. There is a pedagogical process in EE training because the participants are in cadres. This cadre formation is seen within the framework of discipleship. Career stages are available for those who diligently take this training. EE training is packaged in stages that can be obtained by participants who diligently follow each level of training. The training stages are to become a witness, trainer, teacher, implementer, and senior implementer. EE trainers who take part in the training stages have good communication skills, mastery of the material, and also teamwork.

The EE model of evangelism makes the trainer the center and source of the gospel message. Evangelism that is "sharing gifts" is not only giving, but also receiving; not only talking, but also listening. Trainees are conditioned to accept without invoking responses that invite them to share the gospel in their style, language, and also their own experiences in witnessing who the God they know is. There is a tendency for participants to "imitate" the same form of evangelism over and over again as they have been trained, memorized, and also simulated. From the perspective of education and adult learning, evangelism should no longer be dominated by indoctrinating models but rather be dialogical and transformative.

In addition, I pay special attention to the follow-up section of EE. In this section, participants are asked to fill out the spiritual birth certificate in the tractate. The measure for spiritual newness is spiritual activity, such as reading the Bible, communicating with God through prayer, attending services every Sunday, attending fellowship, and also being a witness. This follow-up part is the part that needs to be criticized because evangelism can be trapped in strategies that are oriented towards instant results and not the process of conversion as *metanoia* or life transformation. The measures used are also quantitative measures with an emphasis on the vertical relationship to God. The follow-up section of EE has less emphasis on quality of life and its impact on horizontal relations for others and the rest of creation.

Fourth, there is a tractate with a story approach. The existence of illustrations, especially stories told to guide listeners or evangelism training participants to the gospel story, is interesting for participants. Based on my observations, the narratives in the EE tractate contain more illustrative narratives than the gospel narrative itself. The illustrative narrative supports the main narrative, namely the gospel message to be conveyed. In addition, although easy to understand, these narratives are foreign to local people. Even though EE books experience technical changes, the narrative, story, or illustrations used remain the same.

Evangelism as a testimony values a person's experience of faith as a living narrative that testifies to God and his work in the world. Even though EE contains many narratives and illustrations, there is no space for training participants to tell stories about their life experiences as living testimonies.

The EE model of evangelism provides space for women to be involved in evangelism. From my observations, the participants, trainers, and even the actors who demonstrate the simulation videos are mostly women. However, evangelism is sufficient not only for the presence and active involvement of women but also for opening up space for respect for the experiences and voices of women who become testimonies about the God they believe in. These testimonials can be subjective, local, and communal. Therefore, EE's strategy of "imitating" and "repeating" existing narratives has the potential to hide a distinctive and unique testimony of women. Women's struggles for justice and equality, as part of involvement in social transformation and a form of witness to God, are important narratives in evangelization as a way to live. Women's participation in the EE model already exists, but testimonial spaces for women to witness to God have not been accommodated.

The EE evangelism model is attractive to BNKP members because it offers a strategic, practical approach. However, this model of evangelism does not yet provide space for women's testimonies of God, both in the realm of proclamation and as a lifestyle.

Analysis Based on Bevans and Schroeder's Theological Paradigm

To analyze EE's theology of evangelism, I use Bevans and Schroeder's paradigm categories in *Constants in Context: A Theology of Mission for Today* to find types of EE theology. According to Bevans and Schroeder, three categories of theological paradigms can be used to understand evangelism and mission. The first type is evangelism as a soul-saving or church expansion strategy. The second type is evangelism as the discovery of truth. The third type is evangelism as a commitment to liberation and social transformation. These three categories are used as categories in evangelism to analyze the main theological themes of EE, namely heaven, grace, sin, God, and faith.

Heaven

The EE model's theological view of evangelism begins with an eschatological study through two diagnostic questions. The first question is "Do you know for sure that you will be with God in heaven?" This question leads to the recognition that no one knows when and how he/she will die. Whatever the answer to this question will be reached by a second question, "How would you answer if God asks, why should I allow you to enter my heaven?" The answer to this question has been anticipated beforehand because most people will answer that good deeds will take someone to heaven. These good deeds include persevering in prayer, not doing evil, obeying religious teachings, and so on. Based on EE's theological view of evangelism, good deeds do not automatically get someone into heaven. Entering heaven can be obtained only by God's grace.

The EE model emphasizes the importance of heaven as a destination after human death. Discussions about heaven connect the Nias people with beliefs in tribal religions in the past. In this belief, heaven is known as *Teteholi Ana'a*, the kingdom above the sky.[30] *Teteholi Ana'a* is believed to be the place of origin of the ancestors of the Nias people. After death, humans will return there. The spirits of deceased ancestors are believed to give blessings, and humans will also return to the spirits of their ancestors in *Teteholi Ana'a*. The term *Teteholi Ana'a* has long disappeared from everyday use. This term is also not used in the Nias language Bible as a translation for heaven. "Heaven" is translated in Nias as *sorugo* or *banua furi* (the place to come).

The meaning of life after death is an important issue in the lives of the Nias people. The topic of life after death in the EE model is the entry point that connects the people of Nias to the search for the meaning of life after death. This shows that there is a legacy of spiritual-cultural imagination that makes Niasan people simply accept EE's theology of heaven. However, EE has an eschatological concept that is different than the religious beliefs of Nias ethnics in the past.

30. Gulö, *Benih yang Tumbuh XIII*, 271.

Based on the theological paradigm categories of Bevans and Schroeder's evangelism, EE focuses on the eschaton, namely the end of time as the goal and end of human history.[31] Such eschatology is futuristic and deeply personal. There are four important things in this model of eschatology, namely death, judgment, heaven, and hell. Because this model of eschatology is future oriented, the world and human history become less important in God's salvation scheme. The current period is best used as a preparation period to look for as many "lost ones" (those who have not yet believed in Jesus Christ and become Christians) as possible.

RMG missionaries with the spirit of Pietism in the past upheld this eschatological understanding so that evangelism activities became a strategy to get results, namely as many people as possible became Christians because the end times would soon come. This immediacy is important so that the majority of people during the judgment period do not receive punishment from God and do not go to hell.

Based on eschatological understanding, EE theology falls into the first type of category, namely evangelism as a strategy to save as many souls as possible. This is shown by "multiplication," which is the motif and also the goal of the EE model. This model is also similar to the initial strategy of RMG missionaries in the past in Nias, with personal conversion and the number of converts being a measure of the success of evangelism.

The implication of this model of eschatological understanding for evangelism is an excessive emphasis on life after death and a lack of attention to life in the present. This has an impact on the lack of evangelical commitment to issues of social transformation today.

The emphasis on the success of evangelization on the number of people baptized as Christians also marginalizes the narratives of missionary women in the past. The work of baptizing is the work of male missionaries or male pastors. As a result, measures of evangelistic success do not take into account evangelism carried out by women, because women missionaries in the past did not carry out baptizing work.

Grace

In the EE model, the topic of heaven ends with a question about the measure of a person's goodness so that he/she is worthy of going to heaven. This measure of goodness leads to a discussion of grace. All human goodness

---

31. Bevans and Schroeder, *Constants in Context*, 42.

is never enough or perfect because humans are essentially sinful creatures and can be saved only by grace.

In discussing grace, EE's theological view appears to equate heaven with eternal life, which is directly connected to God's grace. In the tractate *Do You Know For Sure*, it is stated that "heaven or eternal life is the gift of God."[32] Based on the Bible, "the gift of God is eternal life in Christ Jesus our Lord" (Rom 6:23b).[33] According to EE, heaven or eternal life is not obtained through human effort. Grace is like a gift that humans do not deserve. God gives gifts for free without having to pay for anything, either through worship, good deeds, or charity.

Evangelism is the witness and proclamation of God offering the gift of salvation. The gift of salvation according to the EE model is not salvation received in this world but salvation that is oriented towards eternal life after death and also beyond human history in the present. This gift is also personal and can be received only by individuals. Jesus Christ, who saves, is seen as a personal Savior. The gift of salvation becomes internal and spiritual, and brings personal transformation.

Evangelism with an understanding of grace that is oriented towards eternal life places greater emphasis on the importance of life after death. This has an impact on missions that ignore safety issues in this world, which are connected to structural, political, and cosmic issues. Evangelism is seen as having nothing to do with physical and mental health or political and social liberation.

The gift of salvation in evangelism should be understood holistically and embrace both material and spiritual dimensions. This gift of salvation is comprehensive, integral, total, and universal, as both personal salvation in Christ Jesus and salvation on earth through the realization of economic justice, liberation, and human solidarity.

Sin

According to EE, grace as a gift is not obtained by everyone because it is hindered by sin. Sin is a violation of God's laws such as murder, adultery, anger, deceit, evil thoughts, lust, not doing good—and even human indifference towards God is understood as sin. To support this view, the EE tractate explains an analogy about the number of human sins. If humans

32. Kennedy, *Apakah Anda Tahu*, 3.
33. Kennedy, *Apakah Anda Tahu*, 4.

committed only three sins a day, that would mean that in one year there would be more than one thousand sins. If humans are given eighty years to live, that means there are eighty thousand sins. With that many sins, is it possible for us to be worthy of going to heaven?[34]

EE's view states that sinful humans cannot possibly save themselves. Good deeds cannot save humans from sin, because God's requirements are perfect. This view is explained through the illustration of ten eggs. When these eggs were broken and placed in a container, the last egg turned out to be rotten. The rotten egg contaminated all the good eggs. Thus a single sin has polluted all human goodness. As a result, humans are not worthy of entering heaven. So with effort alone, humans can't enter heaven because of sin.[35]

EE's view of anthropology is very negative so any good human deeds cannot lead humans to perfection. The illustration of a rotten egg contaminating other eggs in the container shows human imperfection in any case before God in working for his salvation. This understanding fits the theological paradigm of evangelism as saving souls. According to this type, although humans were created in the image of God, sin has made humans lose their likeness to God.[36]

A very negative view of humans also results in a lack of appreciation for human efforts to be involved and participate in God's missionary work in history. Meanwhile, according to Bevans and Schroeder, God's mission is the fulfillment of humanity toward justice, liberation, and reconciliation.[37] Human efforts involved in God's mission are counted as part of the proclamation and testimony of God's work, including the efforts made by missionary women in the past. The work of evangelism as a form of fulfilling humanity should be appreciated and recognized as part of human involvement in God's invitation to carry out his mission.

God

Based on EE theology, human efforts cannot save themselves from sin. Therefore, only God can save humans. The God who saves has two characteristics, namely love and justice. These two characteristics are explained

34. Kennedy, *Apakah Anda Tahu*, 8.
35. Kennedy, *Apakah Anda Tahu*, 12.
36. Bevans and Schroeder, *Constants in Context*, 47.
37. Bevans and Schroeder, *Constants in Context*, 71.

through illustrations of the nature of God compared to the love of a grandfather and the justice of a police officer. In the EE tractate, it is explained that many people misunderstand God by describing God as a grandfather who emphasizes only love but ignores justice. On the other hand, some describe God as like a police officer who emphasizes only justice, but without love. Both are wrong. What is true according to EE is that God is both loving and just. God loves us with eternal love, but the same God is a just God who never releases guilty people from punishment. The punishment for sin is death, hell forever. In this section, the concept of hell appears as a result of sin.

To support the understanding of God's character, EE wrote a story about a ruler named Shamila.[38] He was the leader of the revolutionaries who overthrew the dictatorial Russian emperor. One night Shamila's bodyguard reported that someone was stealing food. Shamila was furious because their food supply was very limited. So it was announced that anyone caught stealing food would be flogged fifty times in public. Not long after that, the guard reported that the thief had been caught. However, it turned out that the thief was none other than Shamila's mother. Shamila faced a dilemma. If he whipped his mother to enforce justice, his mother would die. However, if he did not punish her because of his love for his mother, the people would not recognize Shamila as a just leader. Shamila must continue to carry out her sentence for the sake of justice. However, out of love, he took off his clothes and ordered his guards to whip his body instead of his mother's. Only by sacrificing himself could justice be upheld and love for one's mother proven. The punishment had been served, but Shamila was the one who was carrying it out. So God did: God demonstrated love and justice through God's self-sacrifice in Jesus Christ.

Shamila's illustration leads to the story of Jesus Christ, namely God who became man. Jesus is the Word made flesh. The man Jesus was sinless, and thus Jesus was perfect. What Jesus did was self-sacrifice to redeem humans from sin. Jesus was crucified to undergo punishment for human sins. As it is said, "He made Him who knew no sin to be sin for us, so that in Him we might become the righteousness of God" (2 Cor 5:21). Before Jesus died, he said, "It is finished." This means that the sin has been paid in full. Jesus died and then rose on the third day. He then ascended to heaven to prepare a gift for humans, namely eternal life or heaven for free. All that happens can be accepted by humans only through faith.

38. Kennedy, *Apakah Anda Tahu*, 19–20.

Based on EE, the understanding of God is explained in the frame of God as a person. Separate explanations regarding God's persons can make people trapped in modalism, namely the understanding that God has three different and separate persons. In addition, in EE's tractate, God and Jesus Christ are mentioned in their roles, while the Holy Spirit is not mentioned at all. Apart from that, the concept of God explained is narrowed to the characteristics of love and justice, while God's character is actually complex and cannot be simplified into just two illustrations such as a grandfather and a police officer.

God in the framework of the Trinity is basic in evangelistic theology. The Trinitarian frame shows the importance of the relationship between God's persons in the Trinity itself so that it becomes an image of human relations with fellow humans in evangelization. The relationship between God, Jesus Christ, and the Holy Spirit is not a relationship of domination, like the relationship between colonizer and colonized, or master and subordinate, but a relationship of perfect friendship or partnership in which the will of one is naturally in harmony with another. In this relationship, obedience follows perfect fellowship (John 15:15). This relationship should also be a reflection of the relationships realized by missionaries in evangelization, namely fair and equal relationships, between both men and women. Galatians 3:28 says, "There is neither Jew nor Greek, there is neither slave nor free, there is neither male nor female, for you are all one in Christ Jesus."

Faith

The final theological theme in EE's tractate is the question of faith. Explanations about faith are included in the form of several illustrations. The first illustration is of the key. The idea of this illustration is that there is only one key for one door. Likewise, with the door to heaven, there is only one key, namely faith. Saving faith is knowing and relying on Jesus alone as Lord and Savior to obtain eternal life.[39]

Another illustration is the story of a man named Blondin.[40] He was able to cross the Niagara River using a steel rope. The first scene is Blondin crossing without a burden and he succeeds. In the second scene, Blondin is challenged to carry a load, namely sand, in a stroller. He also succeeds. In the scene where Blondin is challenged to take humans, unfortunately,

---

39. Kennedy, *Apakah Anda Tahu*, 30–31.
40. Kennedy, *Apakah Anda Tahu*, 30–31.

there is no one Blondin is willing to take on. Finally, there is a little boy who wants to be with Blondin. As before, Blondin is also successful. It turns out this little boy is Blondin's son. He was willing to take part in this challenge because he trusted his father. The story of Blondin is then connected to the issue of saving faith. Faith is not just believing in Christ rationally but surrendering oneself completely to be held by God toward eternal life or heaven.

In the type of evangelism that emphasizes the salvation of the soul, the concept of faith is closely connected to exclusive Christology. Reflections on Jesus's life and work on earth are taken into account but are not as important as the emphasis on Jesus's saving work, namely his death and resurrection. The tendency of this type of evangelism is also a lack of emphasis on the significance of Jesus's life in history and the messages that Jesus conveyed during his life. Jesus's death and resurrection provide a strong reason for this saving faith.

Evangelism as a way of life is closely connected to the work of Jesus and the messages of the gospel. The emphasis on the narrative of only Jesus's death and resurrection reduces the idea of the theology of evangelism that is found through the holistic narrative of Jesus's life together with the people around him. Robert's view of evangelism, which is connected with hospitality in liminal spaces and crossing boundaries of difference, is also based on and found in the daily lifestyle of Jesus, who was willing to meet people who were sinners and different than his people.

Likewise, Lakawa's view of evangelism as social transformation is also found in the journey of Jesus, who brought transformation through his encounters with others. Therefore, evangelism emphasizes not only the final side of Jesus's life but also the journey of his life. For women missionaries in the past, Jesus's lifestyle gave them a lot of inspiration and strength to participate in evangelization. Based on the theological paradigm categories of Bevans and Schroeder, EE's theological views fall into the category of evangelism as a strategy to save souls or expand the church. Analysis of EE's main theological themes, namely heaven, grace, sin, God, and faith, shows that EE is very oriented towards vertical salvation and places little emphasis on evangelism as social transformation.

Analysis Based on the Lens of *Together Towards Life: Mission and Evangelism in Changing Landscapes*

Together towards Life: Mission and Evangelism in Changing Landscapes (*TTL*) is a document produced by the World Council of Churches (WCC) in 2012. The invention of *TTL* was motivated by the need for a firm statement of the church's ecumenical position in determining the vision, concept, direction, and new practices that changed the landscape of missions and evangelism in the twenty-first century. *TTL* is a document that specifically discusses evangelism and missions today. *TTL* provides a theological basis for evangelism that originates from the mission of the Trinitarian God in a dynamic and equal relationship. As an ecumenical document that understands evangelism as a mission paradigm, *TTL* challenges churches to formulate their theology of evangelism.

TTL and *EE* are two documents that are characteristically different. *TTL* contains theoretical theological views on mission and evangelism, while *EE* is a document that is more practical and strategic. However, *EE* material can be analyzed from a *TTL* lens in a comparative-compatible method, because *EE* material also contains natural theological views on evangelism. At this level, *TTL* becomes a lens for analyzing *EE*'s views on evangelism.

There are five parts analyzed based on the *TTL* lens, namely *EE*'s view of the relationship between evangelism and mission, the theological basis of evangelism, actors of evangelism, models of evangelism (meaning of discipleship), and views on other beliefs and cultures. At the end of this section, *TTL* and *EE* will also be criticized based on an assessment of whether these two documents encourage respect for women's narratives in evangelism or vice versa, whether *TTL* and *EE* pay less attention to the history of women in evangelism.

Views on the Relationship between Evangelism and Missions

According to *TTL*, evangelism is one paradigm of God's broad mission. *TTL* recognizes that each church has its understanding of evangelism. Some understand evangelism as an invitation to personal conversion to a new life and acceptance of Jesus. Some define evangelism as solidarity with the oppressed and proclaiming testimony through church presence. *TTL* does not offer a view that is superior to others. However, based on this document, evangelism contains elements of testimony and the goal of social transformation.

When compared with *TTL*, the EE document emphasizes the goal of evangelism on multiplication. The term *explosion* is connected with the word *dunamis* (Greek), which according to the EE document is defined as the power of God that encourages the multiplication of discipleship and the growth of the local church spiritually, numerically, and organizationally. There is an urgent need to convey the truth contained in the Gospels. Evangelism is understood as the "Great Commission" based on Matt 28:19–20. An important keyword in the EE document is the "multiplication" of students. For students who have been trained, they are tasked with passing on the evangelism relay with the same strategy to others.[41]

According to *TTL*, the concrete form of evangelism is testimony (Greek: *martyria*), namely the act of communicating the entire gospel to all people throughout the world.[42] Evangelism is a mission activity that unwaveringly affirms the centrality of the incarnation, suffering, and resurrection of Jesus Christ without limiting God's gift to the world. The good news is shared with anyone who has not heard it, and everyone is "invited" to experience life with Christ. At this point, *TTL* shares the same spirit as *EE* in that it also aims to communicate the gospel throughout the world.

The difference between *TTL* and *EE* lies in orientation. Based on *TTL*, evangelism does not make numbers the main orientation. The main problem with the concept of multiplication in *EE* is the possibility of constricting evangelism to an instrument of Christianization. For a long time, Christian life has been expected to have "fruit," namely an orientation towards results or numbers, while the process of becoming a disciple is not the same for all believers. The goal of multiplication in *EE* reduces the meaning of the process of becoming a student to a mere matter of numbers. Orientation to numbers can lead to interpreting evangelism as mere proselytism.

Basic Theology of Evangelism

The *TTL* document declares the Trinitarian God is the basis for evangelical theology. God the Trinity is God the Creator, Redeemer, and Sustainer of all life.[43] God is described as the God who protects and renews life in all its

---

41. Kennedy, *Multiplikasi*, 68–69.
42. WCC, *Together towards Life*, §80.
43. WCC, *Together towards Life*, §1.

fullness. Mission is the *missio Dei*, which begins with the work of creation, acts of love, and reconciliation with all creation.[44]

Belief in the Trinitarian God leads to the concept of just and equal relationships as an important principle and value in evangelism. This relationship is manifested in the concept of evangelism as "sharing the gift" of our faith with others with confidence and humility. Evangelism is also understood as an "invitation" to undergo discipleship in the Holy Spirit, which leads to life.[45] The understanding of evangelism as "sharing and invitation" is in sharp contrast to the motives of preaching the gospel for domination.

If read from the *TTL* lens, *EE* does not pay special attention to the concept of just and equal relations in evangelism. This condition can be rooted in a concept of the Trinitarian God that is not seen in a just and mutual relationship. In the second point of *EE*'s statement of faith, it is stated that there is one God, who exists personally in three persons: the Father, the Son, and the Holy Spirit.[46] The Trinity of God is understood as individuals in their respective roles in linear history.

In *TTL*, belief in the Trinitarian God leads to the concept of just and equal relationships and is an important value in evangelism. This relationship concept is different than the strategy in *EE*, namely building friendly relationships, but does not aim to build mutual, just, and equal relationships. Friendship in EE documents is understood as the entry point for EE evangelism. This can be seen from the steps offered, namely starting the conversation with a general discussion followed by questions about spiritual background, spiritual activities, and personal testimony. The main problem with this friendship relationship model is the motivation that can be trapped in impure friendship relationships.

Missionary

Based on *TTL*, the actor of evangelization is God (*missio Dei*) who also invited every believer to witness the good news. The church is God's instrument, which is animated by the Spirit of God to participate in witnessing to the Trinity of God. *TTL* states that the actor of evangelism is the Trinitarian God, who calls the servants to proclaim the good news to all humankind

---

44. WCC, *Together towards Life*, §19.
45. WCC, *Together towards Life*, §83.
46. Kennedy, *Multiplikasi*, 3.

and creation, especially to people who are oppressed and suffering, namely those who long for the fullness of life.[47]

In EE, the church or individual is an actor of evangelization. In the EE document, it is stated that the local church is the operational basis that God has appointed for evangelistic activities throughout the world.[48] Every true believer receives a commission from Christ to preach the gospel to all creatures and make them God's disciples. Inexperienced EE trainers are also enabled to share the gospel through involvement in discipleship groups under the guidance of experienced trainers.

Evangelism Model

TTL specifically proposes the "Evangelism in Christ's Way" model. This model is not a practical and technical form of evangelism but contains the principles of evangelism as practiced by Jesus Christ. To be authentic like Christ, evangelism means sharing the good news in word and deed. Authentic evangelism is guided by life-affirming values as stated in the joint statement "Christian Witness in a Multi-Religious World: Recommendations for Conduct." These values include: rejecting all forms of violence and discrimination by religious authorities; affirming religious freedom; respecting all humans and human culture by rejecting patriarchy, racism, and the caste system; and building mutual and understanding interfaith relationships, as well as reconciliation and work together for mutual prosperity.[49]

If analyzed from a *TTL* perspective, EE does not offer principles but rather direct technical strategic steps for evangelism, which are packaged through tractate story illustrations, pictorial illustrations, videos, and demonstrations. There are four steps explicitly mentioned in the EE document. The four steps are friendship, explanation of the gospel, surrender, and immediate follow-up.[50] The intended friendship begins with self-introduction through sharing information about each other's backgrounds and personal testimonies. At the friendship-building stage, evangelists ask two diagnostic questions. These diagnostic questions become the entry point for the next stage, namely the explanation of the gospel. At the stage of explaining

47. WCC, *Together towards Life*, §101.
48. Kennedy, *Multiplikasi*, 3.
49. WCC, *Together towards Life*, 14.
50. Kennedy, *Multiplikasi*, 12–19.

the gospel, the preaching contains five main concepts in Christian theology, namely eternal life as a gift; humans, who are sinful and unable to save themselves; the attributes of God, who is just and loving; Jesus Christ, God who became human; and faith that relies on only Jesus Christ for salvation. The next stage is surrender, namely repentance to follow Jesus alone. The final stage is a direct follow-up that encourages someone who has submitted themselves to fill out a spiritual birth certificate. A person who has been born again proves himself/herself through spiritual growth, namely conscientiously reading God's word, praying, worshiping, and also witnessing to others. The multiplication model offered requires evangelists to memorize Bible verses and evangelism illustrations, as well as carry out direct simulations.

For the Indonesian context, which is plural in terms of religion, belief, culture, and tradition, EE needs to consider inclusive principles and values in viewing diversity in society. Technical guidelines for evangelism are important. However, as a model of evangelism, EE requires basic principles and values that are mutually understood so that evangelism does not become a means of dominating, degrading, or discriminating against those with different beliefs and cultures from Christianity. *TTL* offers "Evangelism in Christ's Way," which EE Indonesia could also consider in carrying out evangelism.

The Relationship between Evangelism and Belief and Local Culture

TTL gives appreciation to local context and culture as the locus for the good news to take root and grow:

> The gospel takes root in different contexts through engagement with specific cultural, political, and religious realities. Respect for people and their cultural and symbolic life worlds is necessary if the gospel is to take root in those different realities. In this way, it must begin with engagement and dialogue with the wider context to discern how Christ is already present and where God's Spirit is already at work.[51]

The *TTL* document provides space and respect for local cultures and communities to witness the work of the Trinitarian God in their respective contexts. *TTL* documents take into account these cross-cultural encounters,

---

51. WCC, *Together towards Life*, §97.

whereas EE documents do not talk about cross-cultural encounters. The EE document does not talk about culture because humans and their culture have sinned, so they do not have any role in the efforts and work of salvation, which comes only from God.

Based on the relationship of evangelism to local beliefs and culture, *TTL* is more open than EE. EE's views on local culture can be explored from EE's theological views on humans and their culture. Humans are seen negatively because of sin. All human good deeds cannot achieve "perfect goodness," so humans and their culture cannot save themselves. A negative view of humans is the same as EE's view of local culture and beliefs that cannot be saved. Humans and their culture have been dominated by sin and can be saved only by God.

Response to TTL

TTL can be considered to be a document that helps EE build a more inclusive and ecumenical foundation of evangelistic theology and principles so that EE's evangelistic model is more contextual in Indonesia, specifically in BNKP.

In addition, neither *TTL* nor EE paid special attention to women in evangelism ministry. The concept of evangelism in *TTL* and EE is more general and does not specifically target the issue of marginalizing women's thoughts and the role of women in the narrative of evangelism and mission. In this section, *TTL* is also criticized. However, *TTL* has begun to provide a basis for just and equal relations based on the concept of the Trinitarian God, which is a guide for relations between humans in involvement in *missio Dei*.

CONCLUSION

Based on the analysis of evangelism in the historical narrative of the mission in Nias and then continuing with the analysis of the contemporary model of evangelism, namely EE, I make several conclusions. First, based on the historical narrative of evangelization and missions in Nias, the theological view of evangelization in the past, which began in 1865–1930, was evangelization as a strategy for conversion of beliefs, namely from the religion of the Nias tribe to converting to Christianity. It was only from 1930 to 1965 that those missionaries emphasized evangelistic ministry that was connected to social transformation. When evangelization began to take part in the fields of education and health, missionary women began to get space to play a role. Unfortunately, their narrative has not been published clearly in mission history and BNKP history books.

Second, contemporary evangelism, namely EE, has never been officially analyzed by BNKP as to whether EE's teachings are following BNKP's current theology. There has also been no effort by BNKP to adapt or modify the standard EE materials used since 1993 to suit church theology. Existing EE materials have been simply used in training. I have analyzed EE's theology of evangelism through several instruments, including empirical observation, theological paradigm categories, and analysis from the lens of the church's ecumenical document, namely *TTL*. Based on this analysis, EE shows a tendency towards evangelism as a strategy with the aim of multiplication. The EE tractate receives attention because it offers practical strategies for evangelism. However, in terms of theological foundations, EE must be criticized because it can be trapped in the potential for instrumentalization and domination rather than the goal of evangelism as a way to live and proclaim the good news with the principles of sharing gifts and invitations.

Third, based on the results of my analysis, the theology of evangelism in BNKP, both through mission history and the model of evangelism practiced today, namely EE, shows that there are traces of evangelism being a means of domination of others, including domination of women which results in their absence in mission history. Therefore, there is a need to reexamine the reasons behind the absence of women's narratives in evangelism and also the need to reraise these narratives so that women's voices, thoughts, and roles are included in the evangelism narratives.

3

EVANGELISM AS MISSION FROM A POSTCOLONIAL FEMINIST MISSIOLOGICAL PERSPECTIVE

THEORIES OF WOMEN'S MISSION

Christian Home

ACCORDING TO DANA L. Robert, since 1830, the Christian home has been the basis for sending women to engage in mission work. Based on traditional assumptions, women have a special responsibility to care for the family and children. The domestic role of women is supported by religion and culture, so it is not surprising that in the Christian home theory, women missionaries are given the role and responsibility of "making a home" and being role models for Christian and non-Christian families. For this purpose, the roles of women missionaries in the past were closed to organizing household needs, for example, looking after and educating children, caring for the sick, teaching hygiene, and cooking food well.[1]

The Christian home can be connected to the work and role of women missionaries, especially the wives of the early Rheinische Missionsgesellschaft (RMG) missionaries in Nias. Annamarie Töpperwien, one of the missionary wives in Nias, wrote a book containing the testimonies of the missionaries' wives. Töpperwien says that there is almost no other profession in which a husband is as dependent on his wife as a missionary couple

---

1. Robert, "What Happened to Christian Home."

in a remote mission station.² For example, when Pauline Garschagen, wife of missionary Friedrich Kramer, died, she was praised as a woman of intelligence, experience, and knowledge of practical work. Garschagen was recognized as having a heart for the interests of God's kingdom. Another missionary named Heinrich Lagemann also spoke about his wife, Luise Lagemann, who was with him during difficult times in mission work. In times when it was difficult to get clothes, his wife sewed clothes for him.³ Likewise, the story of Sophie Denninger, the wife of missionary Ludwig E. Denninger, is described as the image of the wife of the early missionaries in Nias, namely a housewife who is obedient, humble, and willing to sacrifice, and supports her husband's ministry.⁴

Töpperwien emphasized that the task of missionaries was to teach and convert, but without the help of their wives, they would not have succeeded. Missionary wives in Nias advanced their husbands' work in at least two ways. First, missionary wives had to be seen as exemplary wives and mothers. Second, missionary wives were also present in service in the community, namely to fellow women and children because they have more access to these areas.⁵

Missionary wives in the past were also often involved in their husbands' difficult mission work. Wilhelm Thomas said that his wife, Wilhelmine Müller, had been with him since the beginning of his mission in Nias.⁶ His wife participated in the visits he made to the community. The presence of his wife became an entry point for Thomas to be accepted because the people of Nias were more open to his wife, who was easy to get along with and also quickly learned the Nias language. In a short time, Müller even began to adopt Niasan girls and also taught them Bible stories.

The Christian home is shown by how the missionaries' homes become homes that are open to accepting the local community. Thomas told how their house quickly became like a beehive where people were passing by. Some came to pick up medicine, some small children stopped by, there were schoolchildren who came to visit, and all bonded with the families of the missionaries with joy. At home, Thomas's wife happily told Bible stories, taught needle skills, taught basic hygiene rules, and even sang and played

2. Töpperwien, Seine "Gehülfin," 59.
3. Töpperwien, Seine "Gehülfin," 60.
4. Töpperwien, Seine "Gehülfin," 61.
5. Töpperwien, Seine "Gehülfin," 72.
6. Töpperwien, Seine "Gehülfin," 72.

as part of mission work in the villages of Nias. Töpperwien wrote that Müller was more popular in Nias society than her husband because she was spontaneous and showed solidarity with fellow women. The people served felt Müller's gentleness and warmth. This is what they call love. However, narratives of the wives of missionaries like Müller are very difficult to find, especially in the literature on the history of evangelization and church missions in BNKP.

There are several things to note in the Christian home theory. First, since the 1830s, the Christian home has become a justification for sending women (wives) as missionaries.[7] This theory is recognized as important for the survival of the missionary family itself. Even though women are given leadership responsibilities in the household, the Christian home places a heavy burden on missionary women as mothers and as leaders who are responsible for being models of Christian "virtue and religiosity" for their children. Missionary mothers have a responsibility to raise their children as witnesses of Christ. In particular, for their daughters, there is the hope that they will also become missionary wives in the future. Thus, the mother creates a good example of a Christian family for the non-Christians around her.

The Christian home theory does not yet use a gender perspective so the mission work that is seen as real is the work of only male missionaries, while the work of women is labeled "helper." Women's work is considered voluntary and unpaid, and understood as activism. This is due to a lack of gender analysis that ignores the specific reasons why women join missions. In contrast, public honor is given to men as leaders of mission activities. In addition, domestic service activities are classified as part of mission practices that are "civilizing" rather than "evangelizing."

Second, the Christian home reflects Western values in marriage such as husband and wife cooperation, maintenance of individual character, and emphasis on hygiene.[8] This theory also shows how local Christians adapted the values taught by missionaries to their context. The Christian home, which is applied to local culture, ultimately becomes a model of Christian family faith. The ideals of the Christian home are the realization of cooperation between men and women, as well as the realization of an ethic that is centered on a strong testimony for Christ. However, this theory must oppose patriarchal culture. The Christian home should encourage the

---

7. Robert, "What Happened to Christian Home," 328.
8. Robert, "What Happened to Christian Home," 331.

realization of the better life promised by the gospel, namely a place where children and women feel safe, respected, and valued.

Nowadays, mainstream churches in the Western world no longer have clarity about the meaning of the Christian home. The idea of the Christian home seems to be a legacy of a prefeminist past that is quite confusing because gender roles and family configurations are depicted as a stable structure. Meanwhile, the mainstream denominations, which also faced cases regarding marriage such as divorce and the birth of children without marriage, caused the Christian home to become unstable. In many conservative Christian circles, the term "Christian home" is associated with the moral decline of "sinful" Western society. Additionally, the Christian home has become a code word for evangelical doctrine and culture, when the family is under male authority and leadership.

Third, the Christian home can still be maintained if this theory is recovered from the influence of traces of colonialism and patriarchy, and contextualized.[9] The Christian home in practice must be assessed and evaluated as to whether it strengthens salvation and liberation through Jesus Christ. To restore the missiological dimension of the Christian home, the focus of evangelism and mission should be on the sources of testimony about Christ in the world (1 Tim 3:15; Eph 2:19–20). From an eschatological perspective, the family is a community that in an ideal sense is a sign of the fulfillment of God's reign to bring about justice, love, and mercy for all of God's creation. In God's *oikos*, there is no male or female, Greek or Jew, slave or free, but all are one in Christ Jesus (Gal 3:28). This vision of God's reign, as exemplified by the Christian home, continues to draw women and men to share in the mission of Jesus Christ.

In the Christian home theory, women have the opportunity to lead in the family by being value creators, especially for their children. The problem is when this model of women's leadership is recognized as a "complement" to their husband's ministry. Müller, for example, is better remembered and contributed more to mission work in Nias than her husband. Unfortunately, her narrative has not been remembered the way her husband is remembered as a missionary.

The Christian home has now become a relevant theory for discussion again, especially in the Global South. The Christian home can work well if Christ is the center of the family, and also if there is dialogue with the local context so that the vision of the reign of God continues through

---

9. Robert, "What Happened to Christian Home," 336.

the partnership of men and women. Evangelism and mission work have heavily involved women, and this correlates with women's commitment to family and also Christianity.

Woman's work for woman

Woman's work for woman emerged as a characteristic of the women's missionary movement in the late nineteenth century. The emergence of woman's work for woman was triggered by the demands of a democratic society that assumes that all women in the world are equal. This theory emphasizes that women are needed to reach fellow women and children in the message of the gospel.[10]

The presence of the woman's work for woman characteristic has provided a broader understanding of the term "conversion," which is no longer just about eternal salvation in the future after death. *Conversion* describes the realization of *metanoia*, namely transformation that moves women towards self-appreciation as valuable creatures and encourages them to be free from patriarchal oppression.[11] This movement also provides space for local women to develop their skills and education.

Woman's work for woman has become a door for women to become directly involved in evangelism and mission work. For Protestants, woman's work for woman has encouraged the involvement of women to become missionary "assistants." This term is a label given to women. Meanwhile, for Catholics, women who work in the mission field are referred to as "helpers" of male missionaries. Both Protestant and Catholic women worked in mission areas as educators, especially for fellow women and girls. They also worked as nurses looking after sick people and orphaned children. Traditionally, the ideology of woman's work for woman has been the key rationalization of women's involvement in evangelism and missions.[12]

Based on the parameters of traditional mission work among Protestants, between those who "send" and those who "receive," the idea of woman's work for woman raises problems. Based on gender-based mission theory, this theory is considered to have caused the perception of gender differences in mission work between men and women. Women missionaries are seen as being able to work only with fellow women, while male

---

10. Robert, *Gospel Bearers*, 7.
11. Robert, *Gospel Bearers*, 7.
12. Robert, *Gospel Bearers*, 21.

missionaries can work for all groups. This situation causes a hierarchy of power between men and women to occur. Women have not been given equal and fair power, including in managing finances or other mission work that requires permission from male missionaries as their leaders.

The woman's work for woman movement can also be seen in the history of evangelization and missions in Nias. Woman's work for woman is visible in the past work of women missionaries in Nias, specifically in BNKP. One of the women missionaries whose work can be classified as part of this movement is Hanna Blindow. In 1930, Blindow was sent by the RMG to Nias as a teacher. Blindow's main goal was to spread the gospel through education. In her first year in Nias, her work produced real results, namely the establishment of a girls' school in Nias in 1931.[13] The opening of this school was attended by the RMG, the Dutch East Indies government, and also the people of Nias. In 1932, Blindow also initiated the formation of vocational courses for older Nias girls. The older Niasan girls were not allowed to go to school by their parents because their labor was needed in the fields to plant rice and potatoes. However, Blindow had great concern for them and wanted to do something to improve the lives of local women in Nias in terms of skills.

In Nias, Blindow worked independently in carrying out the tasks entrusted to her, namely to be involved in education for Nias women so that they too could be introduced to the gospel. Blindow's story is in line with the woman's work for woman theory, which still shows the ambivalence of woman's work in evangelism and missions. On the one hand, woman's work for woman is a door for women to be directly involved in evangelization and mission movements. On the other hand, this initial movement was directed only at services to women and children.

World Friendship

The theory of world friendship in the history of missions began to be explored in 1910. Robert tells of one of the unforgettable moments during the World Missionary Conference in Edinburgh in 1910, namely the striking argument of one of the participants named V. S. Azariah from India.[14] Azariah identified racism and missionary paternalism as major obstacles to Christian living. For Azariah, without interracial cooperation, the mission's

13. Blindow, "Letter to Rheinische Missionsgesellschaft" (June 5, 1931), para. 1.
14. Robert, "From 'Give Us Friends.'"

goal of glorifying God would not occur. What makes mission cooperation possible is the existence of "cross-racial friendship" to realize God's image. Therefore, Azariah emphasized the need for "friendship" in mission work. The essence of what Azariah proposed is in the prophetic voice of the struggle against racism and paternalism that characterized the Protestant ecumenical mission in the twentieth century. Apart from that, Azariah was also optimistic about the coming change by promoting "friendly" relations.

Cross-cultural friendship is a hidden component of twentieth-century mission. Azariah's plea "Give us friends!" is a prophetic voice because, despite human limitations, friendship allows Christian communities to communicate the riches of Asian and African Christianity with Western support through cross-cultural solidarity. For practitioners, friendship is a courageous testimony against the racism of Western colonialism.

C. Y. Cheng, secretary of the Honorary National Christian Council of China, once said that the missionary was seen as having several qualities as a disciple of Jesus, namely as a brother, as a companion, as a seeker of truth, but the highest and most important quality of a missionary was as a friend. Cheng said, "Friend is a big word, especially as it appears in the eyes of the Oriental people. . . . He who comes to us with the spirit of a friend through and through will ultimately win our hearts. . . . We believe it is this friendship, which is another word for Christian love, which will solve many of our mission problems, and will lead the work to a more successful issue."[15] Establishing world friendship was the top priority for missionaries in the 1920s. World friendship is a cross-cultural and ecumenical mission effort involving women and youth missions.

Women missionaries adopted world friendship as the main reason for their work, replacing the earlier theory of woman's works for woman. World friendship, especially among women missionaries, is powerful as both rhetoric and ideal. The credibility of Christian fellowship remains in the concrete and specific cross-cultural friendships between Western women and indigenous Christian women. Most of these interpersonal relationships are invisible to history and buried by the details of institution building, conference reports, and political controversies. The details of the friendship narrative must be traced again as a collection of memoirs and correspondence.

The narrative of world friendship can be found again in the biographies of women missionaries as living witnesses who reveal the role of

---

15. Robert, "Cross-Cultural Friendship," 101.

cross-cultural friendship. What the biographies reveal is how missionaries and indigenous Christians shared a cross-cultural vision of the reign of God based on friendship. Therefore, Christians can pay tribute to missionary friends by writing about them. Although paternalism has no equivalent to what is considered the modern ideal of friendship, the patterns of incarnation and adaptation of missionaries of the past to local people's ways of life were a relational form of mission that was practiced as a mission policy by many German missionaries in the early twentieth century.

Letters written by Dorothea Richter, a woman missionary from Germany sent by RMG, reveal how women in Nias became friends in her ministry. Richter even considered them as family. In a letter written to RMG in 1964, Richter wrote how she was friends with a Nias woman named Amina, who was the head of the girls' dormitory. She wrote,

> There is a pleasant collaboration between us and the employees. This is always a reason to be grateful. Sister Amina, above all, has supported our work internally. Amina is truly part of our family. The two people who help us at home also contribute to each course we hold well. That's how we experience the goodness of togetherness and we don't want to miss out on any of them.[16]

The interesting thing about world friendship is that this theory encourages other and different voices to be heard, especially the voices of local women. Postcolonial experts accuse the efforts of Westerners to represent the views of other nations, in fact not allowing others to speak or have a voice. If Westerners name, describe, and translate, then are the voices of indigenous people heard, or are they just a reflection of Westerners' self-identity?

The postcolonial feminist perspective's suspicion of missions is justified but cannot be assessed as a universal experience in every context. If these postcolonial questions are reflected through the lens of cross-cultural friendship, they can be different. In some contexts, Western missionaries saw friendship as a way to empower partners and indigenous people marginalized by colonialism. Even though missionaries are not free from hidden personal interests, the history of cross-cultural relations still reveals a growing momentum toward the construction of Christianity as a multicultural world religion. Friendships between Western missionaries and people from other cultures cannot be ignored and seen simply as a form of colonial exploitation. In contrast to popular missionary literature,

---

16. Richter, "Letter to Rheinische Missionsgesellschaft" (Jan. 18, 1965), para. 3.

which has used the missionary image as an object for fundraising purposes or scientific theory purposes, the post-World War I missionary ethic of friendship sometimes created other and different outcomes, for example, friendship to the point of extreme self-sacrifice.

Until the mid-twentieth century, world friendship was a strong mission ethic and practice. However, world friendship is little known in world Christianity as a multicultural community. Without friendship as a clear testimony of Christlike love, the injustices and racism of the colonial era might have prevented the spread of Christianity across cultures. Azariah's speech was a complaint, but it was also a prophecy. For some missionaries, lifelong cross-cultural friendships are an important witness against racism and colonialism and a sign of God's unwavering rule. Jesus said, "Greater love has no one than this, that a man lay down his life for his friends" (John 15:13). Jesus's willingness to give his life for his friends was an incarnational lifestyle adopted by some Western missionaries in partnership with Asians and Africans, including people of other religions who were also friends.

In the current context of globalization, the desire for cross-cultural relationships is often a stronger motivation for mission work than for evangelism or social service. Today's missionaries see the construction of interracial and intercultural relations as a means of mission and an end in itself. But in an age characterized by short-term mission service, what is the deeper meaning of friendship? Is true friendship the same as economic sharing, or is the model instead a self-deceptive rationalization that makes the rich feel good about their charitable activities?

A century after Azariah, there is a commitment of missionaries today who go on missions to certain people from other cultures. Do they learn language or develop reciprocal relationships with "others"? Friendship like that espoused by missionaries in the colonial period required a long-term commitment to the people of a particular place. There was a great effort to understand and respect other cultures or religions. There was a desire to live with and place oneself in the service of others. Robert challenges the concept of friendship in today's world of instant communication, especially when concern for others is short-lived and development with material donations is seen as a mission.[17] Sacrifice as a practice of friendship is essentially evidence of the reign of God's ethic of love for all people. Despite the dangers of paternalism, friendship remains the proof and promise of Christianity as a global, multicultural religion.

17. Robert, "Cross-Cultural Friendship," 106.

Partnerships

In the mid-twentieth century, with the end of European colonialism, the trend in mission organizations was toward "partnerships" and "mission partners." This trend replaced friendship as the perceived ethic suitable for the postcolonial era.[18] There were questions at the time as to whether it was realistic to reemphasize "friendship" as a contemporary framework for mission relations in today's globalized world.

World War II hastened the end of European colonialism. The decolonization of the church accompanied the death of European rule in colonial countries and created the independence of new countries on the continents of Africa and Asia. Witnessing the strong cross-cultural friendships of the colonial era is not an adequate symbol for the new age. Personal friendship was no longer a strong witness against racism because the era was marked by revolutionary theology, militancy, nationalism, and social Marxist criticism of the Western economic model. At that time, it was not profitable for local Christian leaders to emphasize their close ties to Western friends or sponsors. In the era of revolutionary nationalism, local Christians who demonstrated strong international ties were suspected of being less patriotic and even accused of betrayal.

Missionary movements adapted to the end of colonialism by embracing the idea of partnership as a postcolonial model for cross-cultural relations. In 1947, the International Mission Board meeting in Whitby identified "partnership in obedience" as a central theme. The founding of the World Council of Churches in 1948 created a formal framework within which interchurch relations could occur. During the 1950s and 1960s, older mainstream denominations transferred assets and projects to their overseas "partners."[19]

The evolving meaning of the idea of partnership is also a source of contention. Western mission boards appear to favor the creation of global denominations as a partnership framework, while some non-Western leaders prefer regional or national approaches to denominations. Western mission theorists, such as Max Warren of the Church Missionary Society, confronted decolonization in the mission field by emphasizing the simpler goal of "Christian presence" over the category of friendship.[20] Postcolonial

---

18. Robert, "Cross-Cultural Friendship," 105.
19. Robert, "Cross-Cultural Friendship," 105.
20. Robert, "Cross-Cultural Friendship," 105.

missionaries need to focus on listening and being present, rather than running the show or acting as spokespeople for Asia and Africa. As originally practiced, the idea of partnership was more corporate, structured, and less intimate than friendship. Colonial guilt and pressure to rectify the past instead transform ideals of partnership into development projects that often lack personal commitment and faith based on ideal friendship.

Francis Adeney saw an opportunity for partnership theory to be developed among women in Indonesia. For Adeney, missions were no longer seen as a West-to-East project. When Adeney worked with churches in Indonesia, she saw that there were opportunities for women to be involved in leadership through collaborative efforts through ongoing partnerships with Western missions.[21] These efforts are based on the collective need of women in the world to struggle to develop the economy, fight the stigma against HIV/AIDS, and provide equitable education for women. Adeney also underscored the importance of learning and hearing Indonesian views and traditions that can enrich Western knowledge about missions.

Women's mission theories, namely the Christian home, woman's work for woman, world friendship, and partnership, show evidence of women's significant involvement in evangelization and missions that has been going on for a long time. On the one hand, these theories show how enthusiastic missionary women in the past were to be involved in mission activities. However, patriarchal culture provides a conducive context for a patriarchal understanding of evangelism so that gender justice is still not ideally realized. For example, the Christian home on the one hand has opened up opportunities for women, especially the wives of missionaries, to get involved in mission work. On the other hand, women's mission work is still labeled as "helper." In the woman's works for woman theory, women have more opportunities for mission work, but their work is still for fellow women and children only. World friendship theory opens up opportunities for cross-cultural friendly relations between missionary women. However, this theory relies more on friendship as an individual experience and still shows a pattern of paternalism that is different than the modern ideal of friendship. Partnership is the preferred form of mission after colonialism. However, these partnership aspirations often become mere development projects and lack the commitment to ideal friendship. These four theories of women's mission have demonstrated women's involvement in evangelism and missions. To be relevant today, these theories need to be evaluated

---

21. Adeney, "From the Inside Out," 184.

and rethought so that they are in line with the ideals of justice and equality for women.

NIAS CULTURAL PATRIARCHALISM AND THE MARGINALIZATION OF WOMEN'S NARRATIVES IN EVANGELISM AS MISSION

In one corner of the BNKP Synod Office, there is a row of photos of missionaries who have carried out evangelization in Nias. Among these photos, there is not a single image of a woman missionary. Meanwhile, based on information available at the UEM museum in Wuppertal, dozens of women missionaries went to Nias to be involved in mission work. Among these women, there are names such as Hanna Blindow, Dorothea Richter, Annamarie Töpperwien, and others. In Nias, they are better known as "sisters" or as missionary wives. The question is why are women who used to do the same mission work as men not remembered as missionaries?

In 2014, there was the General Assembly of the Communion of Churches in Indonesia (CCI). The local committee made preparations. One of them was the construction of a monument to commemorate the arrival of the gospel in Nias through missionary figures. The figure displayed on the monument is the first male missionary in Nias, Ludwig Ernst Denninger. The day of his arrival in Nias, on September 27, 1865, became one of the annual commemorations of the church's liturgical celebrations at BNKP, namely the Day of the Coming of the Gospel. To make the construction of this monument a success, many efforts have been made by BNKP to find Denninger's photo. Unfortunately, the photo was never found. However, the local committee of the General Assembly of CCI in Nias still founded a statue of Denninger in front of the BNKP Synod Office. The shape and the appearance are estimates only. The construction of the Denninger monument shows how much the church glorifies Denninger's figure above other missionaries. There are so many other missionaries who have appearances, including women missionaries, who should also be remembered by the church. They are figures who were present and worked and served in Nias. Some of them remained in Nias until their deaths.

What is the paradigm behind the absence of woman figures from the collective memory of BNKP or the history of the mission in Nias? The absence of photos of women missionaries is the surface of a deeper root problem, namely the reason that causes half of the existing mission memories to be buried. The absence of memories of women missionaries is a historical denial that women also took part in the mission movement in Nias.

Apart from the figures of women missionaries sent by RMG in the past, local women missionaries from Nias need to be appreciated by BNKP. BNKP has local women missionary figures, such as Masrial Zebua, Destalenta Zega, and Yani Saoiyagö. Masrial Zebua was a missionary to the Manobo people in the Philippines. She outlined her work in her book about the mission journey.[22] Women's writing, such as the book written by Zebua, rescues women's stories and narratives from the erasure of mission and church history. The women who wrote the stories of their journey in mission work became the guardians of their narratives from the domination of the grand narratives of mission and church history in Nias.

Primary suspicion must be placed on the patriarchal nature of the church and the culture in which it exists. The church should care for its historical narrative fairly and equitably and remember every figure involved, both women and men. Patriarchy is a system, structure, relationship, and social practice that recognizes the differences between men and women based on their gender, and based on these differences, men perpetuate their dominance over women. Relations of patriarchal domination open the door to subordination, denial, humiliation, and even erasure of women's narratives in history, including mission and church history.

Injustice towards women is found not only in the church or mission narratives in the past but also in Nias culture itself, which is characterized by patriarchy. The characteristics of patriarchy in Nias society can be found in the following evidence. First, the Nias people have a gender-biased, mono-dualistic cosmological view. This cosmology perceives natural and social phenomena as two different parts but in unity, such as: male-female, right-left, up-down, life-death, light-dark, friend-enemy, inside-outside.[23] The gender bias in mono-dualistic cosmology shows an unequal position due to the differences between the two. The masculine part is in a primary position compared to the feminine part, just as men have a primary position compared to women, who are considered to be in a lower position.

Second, the patriarchal culture in Nias places men as the main power holders in public and domestic spaces. One institution where patriarchy shows unequal power is in family life or marriage.[24] The subordination of

---

22. M. Zebua, *Sampah Menjadi Persembahan*.

23. Gulö, *Perjumpaan Injil*, 17.

24. Tong, *Feminist Thought*, 7.

women in marital life can be seen in the division of labor in the public and private sectors, which are controlled by men. Domestic roles such as cooking, washing, mopping, and looking after children are synonymous with women's or wives' work. The role of women is referred to as *sangolay-agö talinga mbatö* (serving the household). Unequal power is also seen in decision-making in the household, which is in the hands of the husband. In addition, the thing that has been criticized about marriages in Nias today is the practice of *böwö* or bride-price. The worst consequence of the practice of bride-price is that women are seen as objects of exchange.[25] Female missionaries such as Hanna Blindow also spoke out against the practice of very high bride-price in Nias. Sometimes the grandchildren still have to pay their grandfather's wedding debts.[26] The married life that Nias women live in a traditional, patriarchal society supports unequal power relations for women.

Third, patriarchal culture views leadership as being in the hands of men. In Nias society, there is a proverb that reads, *Tebai möi saita zimbi zigelo*. This proverb means that a female pig jaw cannot be relied on. The real meaning is that women cannot be depended on or are not worthy of being leaders. This proverb has long been believed by the people of Nias who used to earn their living through hunting, including hunting pigs. In the past, men went hunting while women stayed at home to look after the children. A sign that someone is skilled at hunting can be seen from the number of jaws of hunted pigs hanging on the walls of their house. The jaws that can be hung are only those of male and adult pigs because they have curved fangs so they can be hung. Female pigs do not have these fangs. Nowadays, this proverb is no longer relevant because Nias people no longer live in the hunting era, and Nias women also do not only stay at home for domestic work such as looking after and caring for children.

Fourth, patriarchy in Nias culture is also seen in ownership rights or inheritance rights. For the Nias people, inheritance rights fall in the hands of male descendants because men are seen as *fangali mbörö sisi* (descendant successors). Another reason that women do not receive inheritance from their family of origin is that when a woman marries, she becomes her husband's property and gets a share of her husband's ownership. This view shows that the Niasan women do not have individual ownership because what they own is always attached to a power greater than themselves,

---

25. Harefa, "*Böwö*."
26. Blindow, "Letter to Rheinische Missionsgesellschaft" (Nov. 20, 1952), 1.

namely to their family of origin or later to their husband. Nowadays, for more modern Nias families, daughters also inherit from their parents, although a smaller portion compared to sons.[27] Thus, in terms of inheritance rights, Nias daughters have a weak position compared to sons.

The patriarchal culture in Nias society must be criticized from a feminist approach. Feminism is a movement to achieve rights, interests, freedom, justice, and equality for women. According to Asia Parveen, there are five main points of feminist criticism.[28] First, feminist criticism rejects the biological differences in women's and men's bodies as a reason for women's subordination. In Nias's patriarchal society, subordination due to biological differences is visible. Men are seen as the next generation, so the reins of power and leadership are given to boys, who are considered *fangali mböö sisi*. This subordination due to biological differences cannot be justified even on the grounds of procreation or regeneration, which essentially requires the significance of women's biological role.

Second, feminist criticism takes into account women's experiences as unique and special. Feminism as an academic discipline realizes that it is always bound to context. Therefore, feminist interpretations are not value neutral. The experience of Western women is different than the experience of Eastern women. Likewise, the experience of Indonesian women in Batak land is different than the experience of Indonesian women on the island of Nias. Feminism is shaped by experience in a specific context; it is local and even personal.

Third, feminist criticism sees the need for discourse on language choice as a third option to break the understanding that language is controlled only by men's language, and women's language has long been considered inferior, unclear, and unimportant. The language used in a patriarchal society needs to be suspected and criticized, especially if the language results in subordination and discrimination against women. The choice of language used influences human thinking paradigms and the way they treat each other. For example, terms or titles given to Nias women such as *böli gana'a* (bought with gold) or *sangolayagö talinga mbatö* (household servant) must be criticized. *Böli gana'a* results in the objectification of women, and *sangolayagö talinga mbatö* can have the impact of limiting women's roles to the domestic arena only.

---

27. Harefa, "Perempuan Nias."
28. Parveen, "Feminism."

Fourth, feminist criticism challenges the Freudian understanding that devalues women's sexuality based on differences in the psyche (unconscious). There is a binary view in Nias society that men use logic more while women use their feelings more in making decisions. This view is a social construction. Meanwhile, Niasan women are taught to express their feelings, especially sad feelings. For example, in the Niasan traditional wedding series, there is an important rite for the bride called *fame'e*, which means being made to cry. *Fame'e* is a rite of giving marriage advice to the bride.[29] This shows that the differences between men and women do not just happen but are constructed by society, including through the rites of life. Rejections of women in leadership at congregation, resort (a coalition of some congregations), and synod levels also often use the excuse that women are more controlled by feelings than logic. Of course, this must be criticized.

Fifth, feminist criticism pays attention to the fact that women experience more rejection, intolerance, and subordination in various domains, including economic and social. Men also have the opportunity to be discriminated against by patriarchal culture. Gender bias due to patriarchy discriminates against not only women but also men. However, cases of discrimination are more often experienced by women, including in the church.

Patriarchy in Nias culture cannot be denied as one of the factors that causes discrimination against women and women's narratives in evangelism and church missions. To target these inequalities and biases, feminist analysis becomes significant. Feminist interpretations develop very richly because they continuously self-critique themselves by considering the context and experiences of different women. Feminism in any context agrees that women's voices, thoughts, and experiences must be heard. If in a hierarchical patriarchal culture and tradition women's voices are not heard and are silenced by men, then feminism urges that the space for women's voices be opened as wide as possible.

COLONIALISM IN THE TRACES OF EVANGELISM AS A MISSION

Apart from patriarchy, another layer of power connected to evangelism and missions in the past is colonialism. The Indonesian people were colonized

---

29. Gulö, *Perjumpaan Injil*, 236–39.

by the Dutch East Indies and Japanese governments. The Dutch East Indies government had been in administrative power in Nias since 1824. Even though the mission agency that sent missionaries to Nias came from Germany, the colonial mentality in mission could not be separated from the relationship between Western nations and local communities. Analysis of colonialism in mission studies is important to discover the systems, practices, policies, and ideologies that shaped European colonialism in the past and its impact on the dehumanization of non-Western societies through racial taxonomies, hierarchical systems based on patrilineal lineage legitimized by the church, and so on.

One of the traces of colonialism is racism. Racism is connected to the privileges of white people and the power they have to facilitate social transformation for local communities. This power can take the form of rights of intellectual, social, and financial capital, which makes local communities dependent on Western nations. Racism supports marginalizing people who are on the fringes of dominant social categories. Therefore, there is a need for awareness of the destructive continuity of racism which has also perpetuated the history of evangelism and missions.

Apart from racism, colonialism also inherited a spirit of domination over others. Evangelism and missions in the history of Christianity were distorted when they became instruments of power, even though on the other hand there was a mission to introduce Christianity. In the nineteenth to early twentieth centuries, Christian missions in Europe were strongly influenced by the spirit of Pietism and revivalism. According to I. H. Enklaar, five motifs inspired Western mission services at that time:

First, a sense of crisis caused by the expectation of the return of Jesus Christ as judge to establish the kingdom of God. Second, a sense of duty to carry out God's Great Commission (Matt 28:19). Third, pity for "lost souls" who must be saved. Fourth, hatred of worldly sins, namely adultery and idolatry. Fifth, a great desire to glorify God through testimony. The result of this evangelism was the "conversion" of local people from their tribal religion to Christianity.[30]

The mission goal of "saving souls" was first expressed by Pope Alexander VI in 1493 on the eve of the great expansion of colonial missions.[31] This understanding continued into the nineteenth century and was continued by mission agencies. At the same time, the Pietist movement with a spirit

---

30. Hummel and Telaumbanua, *Cross and Adu*, 72.
31. I. H. Enklaar, as cited in Neill, *Colonialism and Christian Missions*, 11.

of mission targeted the whole world. This movement also understands the mission goal to "save the souls" of individuals from disbelief. One of the successes of the mission is measured by the success of the "mass conversion" of local people from local beliefs to Christianity.

The idea of evangelism to "save souls" took the same form as the concept of proselytism today. According to David Kerr, the concept of proselytism in the Bible and Christianity today has different features.[32] In the Old Testament, being a proselyte was an honor among the Israelites, because a proselyte became a neighbor by following requirements such as circumcision, baptism, and sacrificial offerings. In the New Testament, Jewish proselytes were among the first Christians welcomed as members of the early church (Acts 2:9–10; 6:5; 13:43).

Since the eighteenth century, proselytism has had negative connotations for religious freedom. Kerr compares several meanings of proselytism according to Christianity. For the Roman Catholic church, conversion is distinguished from proselytism. Repentance or conversion is an expression of inalienable religious freedom that must be understood as an ongoing spiritual journey, but proselytism as a compelling mission must be rejected. For ecumenical Protestants, the WCC has repeatedly emphasized that the church has a mission. At the same time, the WCC accepts the criticism that the Christian witness is often distorted by coercive proselytism, conscious or unconscious, explicit or subtle. From Kerr's perspective, the church is called to guard against the narrowing of mission as proselytism. The goal of evangelism is not proselytism but life transformation by the gospel, which changes a person's lifestyle so that they have integrity in their testimony through words and deeds as the example of Jesus Christ.

In the history of BNKP, evangelism with the aim of Christianization has led to denigration and even rejection of local beliefs as part of Nias culture. The rejection of this belief was carried out by the Dutch East Indies government and Western missionaries from Germany who looked down on and considered the original beliefs of the Nias people to be "infidel."[33]

Some BNKP historical documents show a negative response to Nias local beliefs. In the BNKP ministers' training material in 2011, it is stated that the original beliefs of Nias are animism and occultism, which must be transformed by Christianity.[34] The BNKP Pastoral Order in 2012 also states

---

32. Kerr, "Christian Understanding of Proselytism," 8.
33. Hummel and Telaumbanua, *Salib dan Adu*, 180.
34. PLPI, *Materi Penataran Pelayanan*, 84–94, esp. 84.

clearly that if anyone has beliefs in other beliefs, the person concerned will receive consequences in the form of ex-communication.[35] These documents show that the Christian mission is the "conversion" of local "pagan" religions to Christianity.

One of the strategies used to carry out the conversion was to first conquer the leaders of the Nias ethnic, namely the *Salawa*, *Si'ulu*, and *Tuhenori*.[36] When the leaders had submitted, the people under their leadership inevitably had to become Christians and be civilized to suit Western culture. This method is in line with *cuius regio, euis religio*. The conquest of the local leader or government of Nias was also the conquest of its people. If the leader submits and becomes a Christian, then the people will also always follow the leader's beliefs.

The conquest of the local beliefs of the Nias tribe who believed in *Adu* (statues believed to be the dwelling place for the spirits of ancestors) was the elimination of Nias traditions connected to these beliefs. There are local beliefs, myths, philosophies, and stories of the Nias people that can be useful sources for the development of local feminism from the perspective of Nias women. For example, the local myths and stories of the Nias people are connected to Adu and, at the same time, show traces that Nias women have a source of strength within themselves whose existence was recognized in the past.

One of the myths connected to Adu is the myth of the goddess Silewe Nazarata. It is symbolized by *Adu horö* in the form of two figures. The first figure has male organs with female breasts, while the second figure has the anatomical shape of a female body, but its face has a mustache and beard. Peter Suzuki believes that Silewe Nazarata was the highest goddess in Nias society in the past because she had several abilities.[37]

Silewe Nazarata is the creator of the world. She formed the world from the parts of her body. When a human was created, she placed wisdom and understanding in the human body. On earth, she grew rice through a woman, who became her messenger. Silewe Nazarata has the power to act as a mediator between the divine and humans.[38] When the belief in Adu was destroyed, myths such as Silewe Nazarata were also removed from the local narrative of the Nias people.

35. BPMS BNKP, *Peraturan Banua Niha*, §§2–3.
36. Gulö, *Benih yang Tumbuh XIII*, 43.
37. Suzuki, *Religious System*, 17.
38. Laiya, *Solidaritas Kekeluargaan*, 24.

Apart from the Silewe Nazarata myth, there is also a local Nias story about a female ancestor named Nawaöndru, the wife of Balugu Sirao, which is also connected to the belief in Adu. The story of Nawaöndru initially tells how the Nias people continued their lineage, which was blessed by the ancestral spirits through Adu. On the one hand, this story is a narrative that shows how central the issue of heredity is in the Nias tribe, especially regarding finding male offspring. On the other hand, this story features a female protagonist who plays a very important role in the narrative. The power that Nawaöndru has makes her not an object or medium for procreation but rather a determinant. Nawaöndru is the main figure in the narrative, who has central leadership roles in the family and society. She is an *ere*, namely a spiritual leader who connects humans with ancestral spirits. The figure of Nawaöndru is also a wise person and plays the role of determining the law and providing justice. Nawaöndru is the inventor of *afo*, which until now was a traditional dish for the people of Nias that symbolizes hospitality towards others. Another potential that Nawaöndru has is that she is a healer. When she healed her husband, the healing process produced measuring instruments as symbols of justice. To her fellow women, Nawaöndru showed solidarity, to both the first and the third wives of Balugu Sirao. I intend to highlight this story to show that some stories contain the central roles of women in leadership. The problem is that narratives like this have long been buried. The destruction of the local Nias people's belief in *Adu* has also eliminated local stories connected to this belief, including the Nawaöndru story.

Colonialism and missions in the past have been connected. Russell argues that missions were one of the main components of colonialism and cultural imperialism practiced by missionary women and men in the nineteenth century and beyond. The challenge for missions today is to see "God's mission" with new eyes, namely as an act of God "sending" and "mending" the lives and love of women and all those who are marginalized.[39]

THE NEED TO RETHINK EVANGELISM

The problem of unequal power relations in the history of evangelization and missions lie not only in a patriarchal culture. There are other gaps and layers of domination, namely colonialism, which cannot be analyzed using a feminist approach alone. To target the intertwined dominance of

39. Russell, "Cultural Hermeneutics," 24.

patriarchy and colonialism in the history of evangelization and missions in Nias, a postcolonial feminist missiological perspective is needed.

Patriarchy and colonialism have been closely intertwined historically. The end of colonialism does not mean an end to discrimination against women in former colonies.[40] In postcolonial feminist studies, radical criticism of Christianity emerged, including rejection of evangelization and missions, which were seen as the imposition of Western culture and religion on other cultures and religions. Likewise, criticism of evangelization and missions in the past was still gender biased and resulted in discrimination against women. In academic circles, criticism of missionaries as "cultural imperialists" became a whip for the failure of colonial policy.[41]

The term *postcolonial* is characterized by a shift in the analysis of colonialism from historical events to discourses that precede and transcend the traditional time line linked from colonial invasions to national independence movements.[42] Nevertheless, postcolonialism is not a celebration of the end of colonialism but rather an invitation to expose and challenge new forms of colonialism in local, national, and transnational contexts.[43] Postcolonialism offers a framework for recognizing, criticizing, and proposing alternative frameworks of thought.

To be adequate to the study of evangelism and missions, a postcolonial feminist perspective requires mission studies. This is useful for resurrecting narratives of female missionaries in the past and giving hope for more women today to be involved and appreciated in their thoughts and roles in evangelization as testimonies of God and his work. Therefore, the perspective used is postcolonial feminist missiology.

According to Robert, missionaries are the visionaries of modern history.[44] They generally traveled by writing notes about their thoughts and activities, which attracted historians to research the missionaries' archives. However, since 1996, public opinion about missionaries has been divided. On the one hand, missionaries are seen as heroic figures who risked their lives for what they believed in. On the other hand, for many historians of the late twentieth century, the missionary was seen as an ideologue, namely someone who pursued a single goal and had close relations with

---

40. Shital, "Postcolonial Feminist Theory."
41. Robert, *Christian Mission*, 68.
42. Ruíz, "Postcolonial and Decolonial Feminism."
43. Khoja-Moolji and Chacko, "Post-Colonialism, Impact on Women," 1.
44. Robert, *Converting Colonialism*, 1.

dominating forces such as colonialism, imperialism, modernization, or globalization. As a result, the view of missionaries becomes very narrow, because missionaries are assessed based only on the goals of their mission and their relationship with power. According to Robert, the real stories and experiences of missionaries in specific locations and their encounters with the local people who gave rise to the initial conversion in that location tend to be overlooked in mission history. In these encounters, both missionaries and local communities were challenged to experience transformation to form a new vision for the missionaries. If measured from the vision and also the work of service in the field, then the classification of who a missionary is cannot be limited by a person's gender, social class, or nationality. Missionaries are those who have a vision that is embodied by sharing their lives as a testimony to the Trinity of God to inspire conversion, liberation, justice, and transformation.

There are several important reasons to rethink evangelism from a postcolonial feminist missiological perspective. First, patriarchal culture is an obstacle to the realization of evangelism and missions that provide fair space for women. Patriarchy in the local Nias community became more persistent when it encountered church traditions that were also patriarchal. This condition has an impact on the church's lack of appreciation and recognition of women's work in evangelism and missions. One of the serious impacts of patriarchal culture in evangelism as a mission is the absence of women's narratives in historical narratives, especially in BNKP. There are at least two main history books in BNKP that are often referred to, namely *Benih yang Tumbuh XIII* and also *Cross and Adu*.[45] Neither of these books gives fair attention to the thoughts and roles of female missionaries who were present in Nias.

W. Gulö, the author of *Benih yang Tumbuh XIII*, wrote the history of Christianity in five periods, namely the difficult beginning (1865–90), the period of spread (1891–1915), the period of mass conversion (1916–30), the period of church formation (1930–40), and the new era (1940–65). Narratives of missionary women are not found in this book. Meanwhile, male missionary figures get a lot of space in the narrative. For example, Denninger is remembered as the first missionary; Wilhelm J. Thomas is remembered as the missionary who opened the first mission stationary in Ombölata; Friedrich Kraemer is remembered as the first missionary to baptize local people in Hilina'a; Heinrich Wilhelm Sundermann

---

45 Gulö, *Benih yang Tumbuh XIII*; Telaumbanua, and Hummel, *Cross and Adu*.

is remembered as the translator of the Bible into the Nias language; and Martin G. Thomsen is said to be the founder of the first hospital in Gunungsitoli, Nias. In general, these male missionaries were accompanied by their wives, who also worked seriously in mission service. Denninger had a wife named Sophie Jordan, Thomas had a wife named Wilhelmine Müller, Kraemer had a wife named Pauline Garschagen, Sundermann had a wife named Luise Beyer, and Thomsen had a wife who also worked as a doctor, named Margarete Kühn. These missionary wives worked hard together in mission service with their husbands in Nias. The life narratives of these women should be remembered in the history of the mission and church in Nias.

Cross and Adu, written by Uwe Hummel and Tuhoni Telaumbanua, also contains very few narratives of female missionaries in Nias. The names of missionary wives are mentioned but in very minor roles. For example, Pauline Garschagen is mentioned as Kraemer's wife who opened the door to ministry among women.[46] Luise, Sundermann's wife, is also named as a woman who supported her husband's work so that it made progress.[47]

Apart from a very brief explanation of the work of women in missions, appreciation for their work is also minimal and is generally considered less successful than the work of male missionaries. If judged from other factors, the failure in question was also caused by the lack of support they received in their service, both from male missionaries from the West and the Nias community, which was still very patriarchal.

Second, there is a need to analyze the power relations that might be found between Western missionary women and local women in Nias. There is a criticism leveled at the Western construction of a monolithic "third-world" woman and at the same time challenges to white privilege based on the racialization of mainstream feminist theory. For S. Khoja-Moolji and M. A. Chacko, postcolonial feminists also disrupt the construction of "third-world" women as a stable and universal category. This criticism aims to emphasize the heterogeneity of women's experiences and struggles in various parts of the world that have been under a universal category.[48] Postcolonial feminist engagement with the politics of difference not only allows women to pay attention to the various forms of oppression experienced in postcolonial contexts but also points to the impossibility of finding a

---

46. Hummel and Telaumbanua, *Cross and Adu*, 98.
47. Hummel and Telaumbanua, *Cross and Adu*, 99.
48. Khoja-Moolji and Chacko, "Post-Colonialism, Impact on Women," 6.

universal "postcolonial woman." In line with Khoja-Moolji and Chacko, Elena Ruíz also emphasizes the same thing, that postcolonial feminist philosophy is not just one approach and cannot be used universally because it has various forms and practices.[49] For Ruíz, the postcolonial feminist approach is a polygon that moves from shared concerns that cannot be reduced to general terms.

In the evangelization experience that took place in Nias, female missionaries such as Hanna Blindow were given the title *gawe* (elder woman). On the one hand, Blindow received this title because of her privilege as a white woman in Nias. On the other hand, this title tests Blindow as to whether she used the privileges to gain advantage. Blindow did not use the privileges she had to act arbitrarily, but she encouraged the progress of local Nias women so that they would become servants who would be able to spread the gospel. Even when Blindow was not in Nias for several years, she was still remembered and loved by the women of Nias. This was proven after she returned from exile; the Nias women she had previously studied with returned to visit her and tell her about their lives. Blindow in her letters also expressed great joy when she saw that the Nias women who had previously studied with her had succeeded in getting good jobs in society. Through Blindow's experience, postcolonial feminist criticism cannot be immediately accepted as a universal criticism of the relationship between Western and local women. The various historical narratives of the mission also tell different stories. Therefore, a postcolonial feminist perspective requires information from mission studies based on the diverse experiences of Western and local women.

Third, postcolonial feminist missiology aims to rewrite history based on the specific experiences of previously marginalized people and their various strategies for survival. Gunjate Shital emphasizes the importance of a postcolonial feminist perspective that exposes how women continue to be stereotyped and marginalized.[50] By re-excavating history and rediscovering the narratives of missionary women in the past, there is an opportunity for mission history and church history to be written based on the life experiences and perspectives of missionary women in the past in Nias, specifically at BNKP.

The role of women in evangelization and missions in Nias is no longer in doubt. The problem is that women are often depicted as secondary

---

49. Ruíz, "Postcolonial and Decolonial Feminism," 8.
50. Shital, "Postcolonial Feminist Theory."

characters to male missionaries, who are seen as having greater influence in the mission narrative line, while in patriarchal cultures women are seen as having only a supporting role for men. Because of the understanding that women's roles are secondary in patriarchal culture, their narratives are also not considered important to be recorded, written, and made part of the history of the mission and church in Nias.

In terms of literature, feminism pays attention to women as producers of texts that give meaning to the history, themes, genres, and structures of literature. To become text producers, women's voices must be heard. Virginia Fabella and Sun Ai Lee Park assert, "Until women's thought is introduced and their voices are heard, the work of articulating Christian Theology in Asia remains incomplete. God's face will only be seen half and his voice only half heard. If Asian theology is to be introduced in a significant way, then the contribution of Asian women cannot be excluded, but must be an integral part of the whole."[51] Likewise with the local context in Nias. Until the voices of the women missionaries envoys from the RMG and also the voices of local women missionaries from Nias are heard, the history of the mission and the history of the church in Nias will not be complete.

Fourth, there is a need for a new image of relationships between women in evangelization. Postcolonial feminist figures such as Kwok Pui-Lan view the context of women in Asian culture as very different than Western women in at least three ways, namely: Western women come from traditions and cultures where Christianity is dominant; there is a tendency to universalize the experience of Western women; and Western feminist analyzes are less radical and some are still influenced by racism and ethnic orientation.[52] Therefore, it is very important to hear the different and unique voices of women from Asia.

The problem of postcolonial feminism as understood by Fabella, Park, and Pui Lan is the tendency to view the division of the world in a binary way. I criticize the use of binary language in postcolonial feminist discourse because it seems to categorize women in only two worlds. In addition, the binary view creates a tendency to see Western women as so different than the Eastern that it is impossible for women to work together in fair relationships. Meanwhile, relations between women based on experiences in mission work in Nias produce a different story. What drives women like

---

51. Virginia Fabella and Sun Ai Lee Park, as cited in Pui-lan, *Introducing Asian Feminist Theology*, 32.

52. Pui-lan, *Introducing Asian Feminist Theology*, 30.

EVANGELISM AS MISSION

Blindow to leave their hometown and be willing to come to a completely different part of the world, to start a new beginning in mission work that is so difficult, to give heart and be willing to make sacrifices for other women and children who are not their family, and to want to live together with the local community until the end of her life? A postcolonial feminist approach requires explanations or even other theories to explain the experiences of sacrifice to fellow women as carried out by the Blindow missionaries.

Figures such as Gayatri Spivak use postcolonial theory and apply it through a self-reflective approach to analyze the practices in which women are represented in societies that have experienced colonialism. Spivak's basic assumption is that Western scholarship has ignored the diversity, heterogeneity, and overlapping nature of subaltern groups.[53] She offers recovery of women's voices with an emphasis on the relationship of a feminist ethic of care with a postcolonial outlook and develops the premise of a "postcolonial ethic of care."[54] It has a particular analytical way of approaching questions surrounding contemporary global care. The initial blending of the two approaches was based on several things, namely: (1) explicit recognition of the existence of an asymmetrical relationship, (2) linkage of the values of the two approaches in an alternative "dialogic ethic," and (3) existence of a neocolonial gap between the two asymmetrical approaches global feminine concerns. Spivak encourages the expansion of postcolonial theory to connect to an ethic of care beyond conventional boundaries, through values that support a "posture of humility" in colonial encounters, as well as the different experiences of care of women of color that are expanded into neocolonial global care.[55]

Fifth, there is a need to restore the meaning of evangelism, which has been distorted due to patriarchy and colonialism in the past. The *TTL* document acknowledges that throughout history, evangelism has been distorted and lost its credibility theologically and practically because of Christians who carried out forced "conversions" that were proselytism through violence or abuse of power.[56] The *TTL* document offers a model of "Evangelism in Christ's Way" in cross-cultural and religious encounters. According to *TTL*, authentic evangelism is based on humility and respect for others of different beliefs and cultures, while the EE document does not show a

---

53. Spivak, "Can the Subaltern Speak."
54. Spivak, "Postcolonial Ethics of Care," 9.
55. Spivak, "Postcolonial Ethics of Care," 9.
56. WCC, *Together towards Life*, §82.

clear position regarding the actual goal of "conversion." However, the term "multiplication" becomes a strategy to multiply the number of Christians through a personal approach.

The term "conversion" has become very important in the discourse of evangelism and power. Holders of power have the control to carry out conversions to those who are considered subordinates. In mission studies, evangelism is not necessarily equated with "religious conversion" or what is known as "saving souls." The term "conversion" should be understood in a new way, namely *metanoia* (repentance), which means changing habits, priorities, and life goals to obtain salvation, recovery, and liberation. Metanoia is an invitation to participate in God's mission with a humble character towards humanity.[57]

Conversion that is understood as *metanoia* is the work of God in the Holy Spirit, not the work of humans using dominative and manipulative means. It is the Holy Spirit who chooses whom God uses to work together to witness to God through preaching the good news (Rom 10:14–15; 2 Cor 4:2–6), and it is also the Holy Spirit who works to create new life (John 3:5–8; 1 Thess 1:4–6).

CONCLUSION

Women's involvement in evangelism and missions has been going on for a long time. Theories such as the Christian home, woman's work for woman, world friendship, and partnership are historical evidence that women have been significantly involved in evangelism and missions. The problem is that the culture of patriarchy and colonialism in missions has become a barrier for women to be respected and recognized for their roles. The Christian home and woman's works for woman are early theories of women's missions that show opportunities and possibilities for women to be involved in missions even in roles that are seen as secondary. Meanwhile, the world friendship and partnership theories open up opportunities for friendly relations and cross-cultural cooperation between missionary women.

Patriarchy in Nias culture has become one of the factors that causes discrimination against women and women's narratives in evangelism and church missions. If in a hierarchical patriarchal culture and tradition women's voices are not heard and are silenced by men, postcolonial

---

57. WCC, *Together towards Life*, §22.

missiological feminists urge that space for women's voices be given fair respect and recognition.

Colonialism and missions in the past have been connected. Missions were one of the major components of colonialism and cultural imperialism practiced by missionary women and men in the nineteenth century and beyond. This history is a challenge for missions today to see "God's mission" as an act of God sending and mending lives, especially for women missionaries, who have been discriminated against in narratives. This sensitivity must also be possessed by other mission models, including the EE model. Likewise, church documents such as *TTL* must be sensitive to the need for justice for women in evangelism and missions. Postcolonial feminist missiology aims to reexamine history and rediscover the narratives of missionary women in the past.

4

POSTCOLONIAL RECONSTRUCTION OF EVANGELISM

THERE IS A NEED to reconstruct the meaning of evangelism as a part of mission. The first reason is the awareness that evangelism as mission was one of the main components of colonialism and cultural imperialism practiced by missionary men and women in the nineteenth century and beyond. According to Russell, missions in the past were understood as attempts to "transplant" the church and Western culture when carrying out evangelization.[1] In addition, a postcolonial feminist missiological perspective examines how Western missionary women and local women were represented in literature during the colonial and postcolonial periods, then challenges the assumptions made about women, both in that literature and in the views of society. From a theological perspective, mission with a postcolonial feminist missiological perspective encourages appreciation of women who have been sent by God to struggle against patriarchal oppression by witnessing to God's just and equal care for all creation. Unfortunately, women's narratives have not received enough recognition and appreciation in evangelism and mission literature.

The second reason is that evangelization in the past has not fully considered the local context and the possibilities for cross-cultural, cross-religious, and cross-gender encounters to occur. Russell has an interesting view of when Christianity meets different cultures. She sees two possibilities. The first possibility is that this encounter can utilize differences as a

---

1. Russell, "Cultural Hermeneutics," 24.

means of domination over the other. The second possibility is the opposite of the first, namely that encounters become an instrument of hospitality.[2]

Russell shows there are four ways of seeing when encounters with others become a tool of domination, namely: those who are dominant use political and economic structures to marginalize others, teach the oppressed to imitate the oppressor, use identity politics to set one group against another group, and judge people who come from mixed or hybrid cultures. In the structure of domination, others are stigmatized as lazy, stupid, bad, and evil when compared to the standards of white people. On the other hand, meetings with others can also be an instrument of hospitality. Russell says that hospitality to "the other" is God's act of accepting and embracing differences through justice and healing to a world in crisis, which is too frightened to see differences.[3]

However, evangelism will always be a cross-cultural event. According to Marion Grau, there is a complex circle of theological concepts, interests, motivations, and dynamics obtained through missionary encounters with local contexts. She calls the process *circumambulation*, an attempt to analyze the complexity of the history of the encounter between the Bible and local culture. With circumambulation, Grau sees elements of "danger" and "promise" in the encounter and legacy of missionary work. For Grau, the postcolonial mission must lead to a Christian hermeneutic coalition aimed at ending imperial rule and reconsidering the encounter with God/the divine/the holy in the present with the best wisdom from diverse cultural traditions. The idea offered by Grau is the relationship between the gospel and culture. Grau asserts that to consider the gospel free from culture is to betray the complex reality that always accompanies the process of incarnation. Therefore, the encounter between the gospel values preached by any missionary and the local context will always be a cross-cultural event. Recognition of this reality will make it more likely that the encounter will produce creative, not destructive, friction.[4]

In line with that, Opoku Onyinah also offers how to communicate the gospel with the same core message in an ever-changing world. The world today is characterized by secularization as well as the rejection of God and the elimination of religious aspects from many government affairs. Onyinah seeks to see into the mind of God through changing trends

2. Russell, "Encountering the 'Other,'" 466.
3. Russell, "Encountering the 'Other'" 458.
4. Grau, *Rethinking Mission*.

originating from postmodernism. She also analyzes the mindset and attitudes of postmodernism and several strategies that can be used as the spearhead of evangelism. Onyinah argues that evangelism aims to make people disciples of Christ. To effectively form disciples of Christ in contemporary society, the church needs to develop strategies based on specific practical relationships.[5]

Onyinah offers evangelism through art and culture. Evangelism can be done through the arts and culture of the postmodern world. It is amazing how art and culture gain appreciation in society. Onyinah also finds that in this postmodern era, there is a growing sensitivity to context, an appreciation for signs and wonders, a desire for authenticity, an openness to all types of spirituality, an appreciation for subjective experience, and an appreciation for community.[6] The gospel can be expressed in creative arts and postmodern cultural values so that a Christlike life is lived through these media. Art plays a key role in discussing and exploring morality and spirituality. Stories, symbols, names, language, and all the means of communication identified by postmodernists can be used for evangelism today.

Evangelism as a movement to discover the gospel in local contexts must focus on theology and church history in a multidirectional movement. Bevans and Schroeder are of the view that the Christian mission should safeguard, maintain, and bear witness to the constant traditions of the church, and at the same time respond creatively and decisively to the context in which the church finds itself. The mission has a dual focus, namely from the theological side and the church history side. For Bevans and Schroeder, writing church history is not just about collecting facts, actors, and events, but also provides a constant contextual biblical understanding of Christianity and its doctrinal tradition, because the Christian mission is anchored in the faith tradition.[7] The history of missions from the perspective of church history is also observed as a movement that is not one direction but multidirectional. The mission is not seen as simply the expansion of religious institutions or institutional propaganda but a movement to discover the gospel, which is "infinitely translatable," and at the same time the realization of the goals of the mission.[8]

5. Onyinah, "New Ways of Doing Evangelism."
6. Onyinah, "New Ways of Doing Evangelism," 125.
7. Bevans and Schroeder, *Constants in Context*.
8. Bevans and Schroeder, *Constants in Context*, 49.

MATTHEW 28:19–20 AS A POSTCOLONIAL NARRATIVE

One understanding of evangelism in the past was as an effort to spread Christianity in the world. Brian Stanley highlights events that occurred at a mission conference held by Protestants in Edinburgh, Scotland, in 1910. One of Stanley's findings of the conference was the motivation for preaching the gospel, which was based on the understanding that Christianity is a superior religion and therefore needs to be spread widely.[9] Additionally, there was an emphasis that missionary work should be an appeal to non-Christian beliefs rather than relying on brutal acts of "conversion."[10] Stanley identifies two views among the delegates: an ambition for the spread of Christianity and a focus on the world political crisis occurring at that time.[11] After World War I, involving Christian countries, the ambition to make the world belong to Christianity received strong criticism. The emergence of critical voices on mission motivation gave rise to recognition of the shifting balance of religions in the Southern Hemisphere.

Matthew 28:19–20 is often used as a biblical basis that legitimizes the call to be involved in the gospel. Although the final part of the book of Matthew is known as the Great Commission, some experts give these verses other descriptions such as: "the theological program of Matthew" (J. Blank), "the essence of whole Matthew" (G. Borkam), "the most important of the entire Gospel of Matthew" (H. Kosmala), "the culmination of the Gospel" (U. Luck), or "a manifesto" (G. Otto).[12] Bosch is wary of descriptions or slogans like this because they can lead to the risk of distorting what the Gospel of Matthew conveys based on the context. Bosch even considers the separation of this verse from its context as a violation of Matthew's text and its true purpose.[13] The problem is that if this verse is interpreted apart from the background and context of the Gospel of Matthew as a whole, then something is missing from the holistic meaning of this verse.

Apart from that, another criticism of contemporary evangelistic practices is that the gospel is told only partially, so that the stories are truncated, and prioritizes only the stories that are considered the main, climax, or peak of God's work, namely the narrative of Jesus Christ, who died and

---

9. Stanley, *Christianity in Twentieth Century*, 127.
10. Stanley, *Christianity in Twentieth Century*, 128–30.
11. Stanley, *Christianity in Twentieth Century*, 127–30.
12. As cited in Bosch, *Transforming Mission*, 57.
13. Bosch, *Transforming Mission*, 57.

resurrected. Meanwhile, the stories of Jesus's incarnation, which show the side of God who became human in the course of his life, are seen as less important stories to tell.

Narratives in Evangelism Explosion (EE) for example, do not tell the stories of Jesus who was incarnated in everyday life but focus only on the narrative that is considered the pinnacle of the Gospels, namely the narrative of Jesus's death and resurrection. Meanwhile, there is a lot of value to be gained through the stories of the life of Jesus Christ on earth. These stories include the gospel story, which embraces marginalized people, such as women; and also the life story of Jesus, who rejected colonization politically and economically.

Lakawa offers a rereading of Matt 28:19–20, verses often claimed to be the basis of "the Great Commission" for the gospel. Lakawa proposes to understand the Gospel of Matthew as part of a pastoral-missional narrative of marginalized communities. For Lakawa, Matt 28:19–20 cannot be separated from the framework of the entire Gospel, so to understand it requires a holistic understanding of the Gospel of Matthew through a backward flow to the beginning of this Gospel narrative.[14]

Lakawa sees a Christological statement in the Gospel of Matthew that connects all the Gospels, namely that Jesus is the Emmanuel, God who is with us.[15] God's inclusion is not only at the end of the Gospel of Matt 28:20, which says, "and teaching them to obey everything that I have commanded you. And remember, I am with you always, to the end of the age" (NRSV). This verse does not stand alone, but its theme starts at the beginning of the Gospel of Matt 1:23, "Look, the virgin shall conceive and bear a son, and they shall name him Emmanuel," which means, "God is with us." Therefore, Lakawa believes that Matt 28:18–20 is not suitable to be understood as a command or Great Commission but rather as a "mission of empowerment."[16] Jesus accompanied his disciples to be empowered to go and make disciples of all nations by baptizing and teaching. The word "teach" in Matthew's Gospel refers to disciple making.[17] The discipleship that Jesus meant was not only for the disciples he knew but expanded and went beyond borders, to all nations.

---

14. Lakawa, "Menggereja."
15. Lakawa, "Misiologi Bela Rasa," 16–18.
16. Lakawa, "Misiologi Bela Rasa," 16.
17. Lakawa, "Misiologi Bela Rasa," 18.

The context of Matthew's Gospel is important to consider because of the problems of power that were intertwined with religious struggles at that time. Warren Carter argues that Matthew's Gospel assumes the experience of Roman imperial power in almost every walk of life.[18] The power refers explicitly to the world of empire, for example, in narratives involving Roman rule (Matt 2, 14), the payment of taxes to Caesar (Matt 22:15–22), or the crucifixion of Jesus (Matt 26–27). There are times when the reality of imperial power is not explicitly visible. Therefore, the awareness of readers of Matthew's Gospel is needed to recognize the reality concerning power relations.

The reality of power experienced directly by early readers of Matthew's Gospel is different than the experience of readers in other places in different historical periods, so awareness of these power dynamics is needed. For example, the situation when Jesus had ongoing conflicts with religious leaders—these conflicts were not just religious issues but were connected to other issues. There are several reasons given by Carter. First, religious leaders are members of the upper class, namely part of the ruling elite who are committed to perpetuating the social order in society, because they also benefit and experience the benefits and privileges of it. Second, religious issues were not separate from social and political issues in the imperial world. The conflicts that occur have multiple dimensions. Based on these factors, it can be concluded that religious leaders are part of the ruling elite, and religious issues are related to social, political, and economic issues. This was what Jesus was concerned about in his time. Jesus conflicts with representatives of the ruling class, namely people who want to perpetuate this oppressive social structure. These rulers also understood that Jesus's mission was to carry out social transformation. Jesus's mission was seen as an attack on their power, wealth, and status.[19]

Carter argues that the Gospel of Matthew challenges the Roman Empire in two ways. First, the Gospel of Matthew presents a social challenge that offers a different vision and experience of community interaction. Rather than being hierarchical, exploitative, and exclusive, the community creates a society that is inclusive, egalitarian, generous, and loving toward others. This social vision is rooted in the organizational structure and expression of the theological tradition and worldview of the Matthew community. Therefore, the presence of the Gospel of Matthew challenges

---

18. Carter, *Matthew and Empire*, 35.
19. Carter, *Matthew and Empire*, 35.

imperial theology or a worldview that claims that the world belongs to it. The Gospel of Matthew also refutes the claim that the emperor is a divine agent to distribute blessings to the world. It challenges the perception that Rome should rule the world and rejects Rome's claim to sovereignty as well as a vision of Roman social interaction that benefits the few and causes hardship for the majority. Thus, the Gospel of Matthew offers a concept of the kingdom of God that reconfigures human social interactions.[20]

Carter also emphasizes that the Gospel of Matthew challenges the claims of imperial theology, which understands that empires and emperors are representatives or intermediaries of the divine on earth. Jesus challenged the establishment claiming that the emperor represented divine sovereignty, presence, and medium to ensure the well-being of society. The Gospel of Matthew presents a Jesus who overthrew imperial theology and gave legitimacy to an alternative community with a new lifestyle.[21]

In Matt 1:23, there is a description of the appearance of a situation that on the one hand is dominated by imperial power and on the other hand shows the baby Jesus as a sign of resistance and hope for people who are under imperial control. Within the Roman Empire, God sent Jesus on a mission to save people. Part of that mission is to embody God's presence and leadership. Starting from 4:18–22, there is a narrative when Jesus forms a community by calling people to follow him as a manifestation of the figure of the kingdom of God. The kingdom requires and takes form through a nation or people. The kingdom of God is expressed in this community. Jesus's mission is for everyone to encounter the kingdom of God and join this community (4:19). In 10:8, Jesus again sends his disciples on a mission: Heal the sick, raise the dead, cleanse lepers, and cast out demons. Healing is Jesus's mission for people trapped in everyday misery, so they can change their lives, experience new social interactions, and participate in inclusive communities.

At the end of the Gospel, the resurrected Jesus commands his disciples, "Go therefore and make disciples of all nations" (Matt 28:19a). Jesus once again offers a different experience of social reality. This command is accompanied by instructions to go on mission or to teach (10:7; 28:19–20). Each mission not only requires powerful action and provides new social attachments but also explains the proclamation of the importance of these actions with God's purposes. Proclamation is not only about influencing

20. Carter, *Matthew and Empire*, 53.
21. Carter, *Matthew and Empire*, 57.

people to live and act in certain ways but also about influencing people to think, understand, and perceive the gospel in certain ways.[22]

Matthew 18 is generally known as Jesus's "community discourse," because in this chapter Jesus teaches his disciples about communal interaction and the responsibilities that come from the kingdom of God (18:1–4, 23). The community of followers of Jesus must be characterized by service, compassion, reconciliation, and forgiveness. The community of Jesus's followers remains open for anyone to participate. It is a community that is inclusive and compassionate and offers distinctive alternatives to structures and practices. Only then is the presence of Jesus encountered.[23] The community is not characterized by domination but rather by service to one another and new patterns of kinship (20:25–28). Jesus's community was not formed based on considerations of wealth, gender, status, or ethnicity but based on being children of God (5:9, 45). Households are formed concerning God's will (12:46–50), not by the pattern of patriarchal domination of husbands over wives. Men do not have the right to exploit women due to economic vulnerability or other reasons. In the reign of God, no man should exercise "fatherly" authority (23:9), but all disciples are children (19:13–15) and servants (20:25–28).[24]

Apart from the introduction to the context of Matthew's Gospel and the interweaving of power that exists within the community, a significant thing in Matthew's Gospel is the description of to whom God is known in Matthew's community. In Matt 28:20 it is written, "And remember, I am with you always, to the end of the age." According to Lakawa, the phrase "I am with you" leads to the question of who is "I" or who is the God that the believing community believes in the Gospel of Matthew. In the gospel message, "who God is" is the main core of the message to be preached. So, the focus of the initial gospel message was not merely on to whom the gospel was preached but rather on who is God and which kind of God was to receive witness.

Emmanuel means the presence of God, the presence of salvation that liberates from imperial powers such as Egypt (Deut 31:23), Assyria (Isa 7–8), and Babylon (Isa 41:10; 43:5). Emmanuel is manifested in Jesus. The presence of God in Jesus appears in Matt 18:20, namely in the context of the community of disciples who gathered to pray. In this gathering, Jesus's

---

22. Carter, *Matthew and Empire*, 52.
23. Carter, *Matthew and Empire*, 65.
24. Carter, *Matthew and Empire*, 127.

presence was encountered. There is an implicit contrast to the kingdom in the narrative of God's presence. Matthew 18 claims that God's presence is not found in domination and is opposed to the hierarchical society established by Rome's elite and economically exploitative military forces. Rather, God is present in an inclusive community of disciples. How important it is to understand the God who accompanies his people can be found by tracing the narrative and previous verses in the Gospel of Matthew, namely 16:15–16, when Jesus asked, "But what do you say that am I?" Simon Peter answered, "You are the Messiah, the Son of the living God!" Peter's statement was a confession of faith in Jesus Christ as the Son of God. This statement is also Peter's testimony and also the message he wants to bear witness to the world. Because of his genuine belief in what he believed, Peter did not experience fear in testifying.

Firmness in what is believed does not make the messenger of the gospel doubt and fear what he is about to witness. Matthew 14:27 says, "Take heart, it is I [*ego eimi*]; do not be afraid!" It is God who reveals. It is God who has first made a mission to introduce who God is to the world so that anyone in the future who also witnesses who God is will be those who participate in God's mission. The statement that follows is "do not be afraid," resonating with God's inclusion in 28:19–20, "I am with you," because the mission from the beginning was the mission of preaching the gospel, which originated from God, then God accompanies this work and gives courage to the hearts of everyone who preaches the gospel.

It turns out that God's inclusion is found not only at the end of the Gospel of Matthew. It turns out that the God who accompanies him has been the frame of the Gospel of Matthew from the start, embracing Matthew's faith community to be strengthened in their faith. "And they shall name him Emmanuel, which means 'God is with us'" (Matt 1:23). It is interesting that the "God who accompanies" is not only at the end of Matthew's Gospel, but it turns out that from the beginning of Matthew's Gospel, the news about who God is has been witnessed.

"The God who accompanies" is the characteristic of God believed in by the collective community of the early congregation, namely the Jewish Christian community, which was living in a time of sociocultural crisis and was in the process of rediscovering their identity.[25] God's inclusion became very important for this early community because there was God's mission to be carried out, namely in Matt 28:19–20, "Go therefore and make

25. Lakawa, "Menggereja."

disciples of all nations, baptizing them in the name of the Father and of the Son and the Holy Spirit, and teaching them to obey everything that I have commanded you."

Matthew 28:19–20 also connects readers to what God has commanded them to teach, namely God's mission to love the world, especially the least of them. "Truly I tell you, just as you did not do it to one of the least of these, you not do it to me" (25:45). In the end, God will separate and judge each person based on the acts of love done or not done towards the least of the neighbors. The topic of love is central to God's mission. Matthew 22:34–40 is a gospel narrative that speaks very strongly about God's command to love: "You shall love the Lord your God . . . you shall love your neighbor." This command is continuous with the gospel messages before and after it. This shows that the command to love is primary in God's word according to the Gospel of Matthew. This gospel command also speaks strongly in the Sermon on the Mount delivered by Jesus in Matt 5–7.

A holistic reading of the Gospel of Matthew helps us to understand what the Jewish Christian community was struggling with at that time. This holistic reading has very different results if these verses are read and interpreted separately and apart from their holistic context. This is an interesting statement by Lakawa, that the verses that have been taken for granted to legitimize gospel preaching activities cannot be separated from the context and struggles of the initial community where the gospel was first addressed.[26] Reading the biblical narrative holistically helps us to understand the relationships that exist throughout the Gospels.

TRINITARIAN COMMUNITY AS A MODEL OF POSTCOLONIAL MISSIONARY COMMUNITY

The work of evangelism and missions at BNKP on the one hand has encouraged the development of education in the field of theology enjoyed by Nias women. One of the developments that occurred was the acceptance of women's ordination as pastors at BNKP. The first ordination was received by Rev. F. M. Martawati (1978), which was followed by Rev. Ibahati Manaö (1990), Rev. Nur Ziliwu (1992), and Rev. Nilamwati Zendratö (1992). Since then, the number of Nias women ordained as pastors at BNKP has begun to increase. The ordination of women pastors is a milestone in the legality of women's professional status as priests at BNKP.

26. Lakawa, "Menggereja."

The early women ministers ordained in BNKP were not immediately placed in leadership positions in local congregations. After ordination, they were placed as functional pastors in congregations or worked in ministry units. Until now, there is still a gap in the acceptance of women pastors as leaders in local congregations. Local congregations in BNKP generally still prioritize accepting male pastors over female pastors. Some of the reasons are motivated by misogynist reasons. According to the view that is still common among BNKP congregation members, listening to women's voices from the pulpit is the same as allowing women to become leaders. Meanwhile, in Nias culture, women are listeners of men's voices. Apart from that, there is an assessment of the services of female pastors, which are considered less effective when compared to male pastors. For example, female pastors are considered to not dare to go out at night to reach difficult service areas, female pastors who are married and have a family will have children and will often go on maternity leave, or female pastors are not strong in leading meetings because they are more influenced by feelings than logic. Accusations like this often circulate among congregation members, so there are still local congregations that prefer to be led by male pastors. Conditions like this continue to occur among churches and society in Nias. Therefore, the struggle for gender justice and feminism in leadership in the church, specifically in BNKP, must still be prioritized.

Leadership, role, gender, status, and position are relational issues. The relationship between male and female pastors in BNKP is still patriarchal, even though the number of female pastors in BNKP is almost the same as the number of male pastors. Based on data on the number of pastors available in the BNKP Synod Office at the beginning of 2024, the total number of pastors is 671: 335 women and 336 men. According to predictions in the future, the number of female pastors in BNKP will be more than male pastors. This prediction is based on the number of students interested in studying at a seminary, for example at BNKP Sundermann Seminary in Nias, most of whom are women. However, the increasing number of women pastors is not commensurate with their status and leadership positions in the church. In terms of leadership, male pastors at BNKP still dominate important roles and positions, including in decision-making.

Patriarchal relationships do not allow equal and just relational concepts to occur, especially for those who are marginalized, especially women. If women do not have equal roles in leadership, how can evangelism speak about justice and gender equality to foster transformative relationships?

Therefore, a reconstruction of the theology of evangelism that offers fair and equal relations is needed.

The source of Christian theology on just and equal relations is the concept of the Trinitarian God. Trinitarian mission is nothing new in mission discourse. The Trinitarian mission paradigm can be traced to the concept of *missio Dei* as a response to the pattern of mission relations, which was considered still paternalistic until the mid-twentieth century.[27] From a soteriological perspective, there is an understanding that the mission is to save souls from eternal punishment. From a cultural perspective, mission is understood as introducing God's blessings to the Eastern and Southern worlds through the features of Western civilization. From the church category, there is an understanding that mission is the expansion of the church. From the perspective of salvation history, mission is understood as the process of the world being transformed towards the kingdom of God. Previous understandings of mission are very different than *missio Dei*, which offers the concept that mission does not belong primarily to the church or missionaries but comes from God.[28] God is the owner of the mission, and humans or the church are those who are included in God's mission. The basis of the *missio Dei* is the doctrine of the Trinitarian God. God the Father sent Jesus Christ. The Holy Spirit then sent the church to be present in the world. Mission understood as participation in God's sending colored the International Missionary Conference in Willingen in 1952. Andrew Kirk emphasizes that the *missio Dei* in question was none other than *missio Trinitatis*.[29] Bevans and Schroeder also note the concept of *missio Dei* as a radical change from the Roman Catholic church's concept of mission as stated in the *Ad Gentes* document.[30] Humans and the church have been united together with God to carry out the mission of the Trinity, namely the Father, Son, and Holy Spirit.

The problem with the concept of the Trinitarian God as understood by Bosch, Kirk, Bevans, and Schroeder is that it still carries the paternalistic concept of the Trinitarian God and reflects Western theology. Meanwhile, to answer the problem of the gap between the positions and roles of men

---

27. Bosch, *Transforming Mission*, 389.
28. Bosch, *Transforming Mission*, 389.
29. Andrew, *Apa Itu Misi*, 31.
30. Bevans and Schroeder, *Constants in Context*, 292. See also Second Vatican Council, "*Ad Gentes*."

and women in mission and evangelism, a concept of the Trinitarian God that offers just relationships is needed.

The doctrine of the Trinity is seen as a stumbling block to Christian feminism for at least two reasons. First, the doctrine of the Trinity is seen to compromise feminism's concern for the equality of women and men, especially because the relationship between the divine persons is seen to be hierarchical. Second, because God is referred to as Father, Son, and Spirit, the doctrine of the Trinity is seen to reinforce a purely masculine image of God. The exclusive use of masculine imagery in worship or theology contributes greatly to the understanding of God as male. This is a religious legitimization of patriarchy in terms not only of male humans as normative but also of human experience as male.

Catherine Lacugna examines the concept of the Trinity in light of feminist concerns.[31] According to Lacugna, for a long time, the Bible, liturgy, and early church creeds by early theologians such as Apologius, Irenaeus, Origen, and Athanasius understood God the Father as *arche* (king), origin, and cause of all things, including the origin and cause of the Son and the Holy Spirit. This idea of the divine monarchy led to a hierarchy in the position of the Son, who was seen as subordinate to the Father. This tension was resolved by Gregory of Nyssa, who redefined the meaning of monarchy. For him, the monarchy in question is not limited to one person but is formed by the same essence and dignity, following the desires, identity, movements, and return of each person to their original unity. This divine unity implies an association of people who are equal though unique, and not in favor of one person above another.[32]

In the Trinitarian God, Jesus Christ maintains the sole criterion of human personality, and the Holy Spirit animates authentic unity between humans so that personality can be realized. Christian feminist concern is with nonhierarchical relationships based on equal human nature and dignity. Theologically, this condition is rooted in the stories of Jesus Christ. God exists in a communion of equal but unique persons. Biblical hermeneutics is important. Jesus Christ preached about the reign of God, namely a condition when women and men live together in God's new household. The household was no longer under the patriarchal governance of Roman or Jewish society. Patriarchy is not God's *arche*; rather, it is God who rules in love and in solidarity with those who experience discrimination and

---

31. Lacugna, "God in Communion," 87.
32. Lacugna, "God in Communion," 88.

oppression, such as slaves, women, outcasts, and the uncircumcised (Gal 3:28).[33]

According to Lacugna, the political implications of this principle are far reaching. First, the social subordination of women to men is only a logical consequence of patriarchal ideas that place men as the *arche* of women. Feminism and also the revitalized doctrine of the Trinity agree on the equality of men and women and do not agree on the principle that one originates from the other and is therefore superior and normative to the other. Second, the doctrine of the Trinity opposes the iconoclastic nature of all humans based on the political arrangement that one person (superior) has power over many people (subordinates). Third, through the doctrine of the Trinity, there is a new understanding of "intra-Trinitarian" fatherhood. Gregory of Nyssa wrote that God is not male because he is called Father, nor is she a feminine deity because of her gender. God is also not God's Father as in marriage and pregnancy. It takes imagination to abandon biological, cultural, and commonsense concepts of fatherhood in the doctrine of the Trinity.[34]

From the perspective of the revitalized doctrine of the Trinity, according to Lacugna, creation and redemption are not two separate things. Creation entails a history of salvation and redemption that is a movement back toward the authentic union of woman and man. All creation groans toward fulfillment, toward something new. The subordination of women was not part of the plan. Redemption means bringing about and completing God's providential plan, revealed in Christ, that man and woman, Jew and gentile, free and slave would live together as one in God's new household. The church must be a visible sign and witness of the reign of God over all the rulers of the world. Second, the goal of every person is to live in communion with others. This communion is authentically from God so it presupposes equal dignity and also freedom from biological determinants such as race, gender, and status. In the risen Christ, and through baptism, we are no longer known or defined by these factors, but we are new people formed by God.[35]

Christian feminism expresses the eschatological hope of the truth of the union of men and women. In the reign of God, when tears are wiped away, women and men no longer find themselves in isolation from "the

---

33. Lacugna, "God in Communion, 92.
34. Lacugna, "God in Communion, 93.
35. Lacugna, "God in Communion, 93.

other" but are in the *arche* in Jesus Christ, namely living together in harmony in the household of God.[36] The divine *arche* is God's government in justice and equality. This situation occurs only if the reign of God continually refers to what Jesus Christ revealed about it. The life of Jesus Christ contradicts the sexist and racist theology of white superiority. Jesus also opposed clerical theology regarding the privileges of church officials, the political theology of exploitation, economic injustice, and the theology of patriarchy, which is dominated and controlled by men.

The insight of Trinitarian theology should free the imagination without forcing us to abandon our traditions. The essence of Trinitarian theology is to convey the essence of God's heart to be in a relationship with humans; that there is no room for separation, inequality, injustice, or hierarchy in God; and that God's ultimate personal reality is an expression of love and liberation. The mystery of the divine life is characterized by self-giving and self-receiving; that divine life is dynamic and not static. The doctrine of the Trinity asserts that God, in whose name we are baptized, is not a patriarchal Father or a God who makes women "less" than men.

Kathryn Tanner also contributes interesting thoughts regarding the concept of the Trinitarian God. Tanner emphasizes the significance of the gospel story for understanding Trinitarian relations. For Tanner, the key to understanding the Trinity is the human life of Jesus, which shows the relationship between the persons of the Trinity, because Jesus is the Word incarnate. Through the incarnation of Jesus, humans were united and connected to the Word. The relationship between the persons of the Trinity thus includes human beings, all moving together for the benefit of the world.[37] The complexity of the story of Jesus's life, death, and resurrection holds the key to this relationship. Tanner argues a Trinitarian theology that does justice to the world's theological concerns is about how the persons in the Trinity are related to each other.[38]

Tanner presupposes that each person of the Trinity is distinct from the others, not only in their actions concerning the world but in and of themselves. Each person in the Trinity is completely equal to each other in divinity, and for all their differences, they are a perfect unity because they are completely inseparable, both in their being and their actions.[39] In that

---

36. Lacugna, "God in Communion, 99.
37. Tanner, *Christ the Key*, 143.
38. Tanner, *Christ the Key*, 147.
39. Tanner, *Christ the Key*, 148.

relationship, God, the Son, and the Holy Spirit have no interchangeability with each other, and for that reason, they differ from each other. God, the Son, and the Holy Spirit are inseparable equivalents of each other in the way they appear "in" each other (John 17:21). God's love for us is manifested in what Jesus Christ did, like a ray of light that reveals the character of its source.[40]

Human life does not have this Trinitarian form or relationship automatically in and of itself but rather "in" and "through" Jesus Christ. By becoming one with the Word, Jesus Christ gives us a new way of life, and we get it through a close relationship with Jesus Christ.[41] If the human is in the image of the second person of the Trinity, it is because of the human's relationship with the second person of the Trinity. Because humans are created in Christ's image, the second person of the Trinity is the place where humans are connected in the life of the Trinity, namely the position with which humans are identified in relationship with the other two persons. Jesus's humanity is never separated from the Word concerning the other two persons of the Trinity, because all of these persons act together for the life of the world. The purpose of the incarnation is for humanity to enter into a Trinitarian relationship. That entrance was made possible through the incarnation of the Word. God's incarnation was for the humans' benefit and not his own.[42]

Therefore, a changed relationship becomes a primary need for humans: namely a changed relationship for us with the Trinitarian God in the virtue of Christ, whose humanity is tied to the second person of the Trinity. All who follow this new relationship aim for human life, namely for moral truth, the fulfillment of humanity, eternal life, and so on.[43] God, Jesus Christ, and the Holy Spirit do the same thing through the same divine power, but in different, noninterchangeable ways. For example, God appears in the actions of Jesus Christ; and Jesus Christ appeared in God's mission for us. This relationship is reciprocal: co-inherence or co-appearance.[44] Each person of the Trinity can be one and equal while retaining their distinctiveness.[45]

40. Tanner, *Christ the Key*, 151.
41. Tanner, *Christ the Key*, 141.
42. Tanner, *Christ the Key*, 144.
43. Tanner, *Christ the Key*, 145.
44. Tanner, *Christ the Key*, 154.
45. Tanner, *Christ the Key*, 155.

The Trinitarian relationship pattern makes humans not just reproduce or imitate it but become part of it. Humans were created by God to be in the image of Jesus Christ as was done through the power of the Holy Spirit who resides within them. God's intention for humanity was fulfilled when the Holy Spirit became ours in a new way, in the virtue of which humanity we became God's in Jesus Christ.

God sent Jesus Christ on a mission that involved his incarnation on earth for our good. This mission culminates in the sending of Jesus Christ to us at the moment of his death, resurrection, and ascension back to God. Jesus Christ came from God, came down or was sent to us into the world (John 3:13, 16–17, 34; 5:36; 6:29, 33, 38–39, 57; 7:28–29; 12:44–45, 49; 17:7–8; and so on), in solidarity with our suffering (Heb 4:15; Phil 2:6–7), interceding for God's good will for us (Jas 1:17), reconciling us to God (2 Cor 5:18–19), offering God's mercy and forgiveness (Mark 10:47–8; Luke 5:20–4; 7:47–8; Matt 9:2; 20:30), heals us of our weaknesses, and brings us into harmony with God's good intentions for human life. Jesus Christ was full of God, received everything that belonged to God (John 3:35; 17:9–10; Matt 11:27; Luke 10:22), giving humans access to God (Matt 11:27; Luke 10:22; John 1:18; 6:45–46; 14:6–7, 9), and making God's work present in his own life and mission (John 5:30; 6:38, 57), as well as being fully dedicated to and trusting in God's will despite all the struggles and difficulties that commitment brings.

God's mission involves giving us the Holy Spirit. The Holy Spirit is one of the gifts that Jesus Christ gave us from God (Luke 11:11–13). By bestowing the Spirit, God's life-giving mission continues through the intercession of Jesus Christ (John 14:26; 15:26). With the same gift of the Spirit that came from God to us, Jesus Christ returned to God (John 6:62; 7:33; 13:1, 3; 20:17; etc.). With God's mission, Jesus was sent as a way to completion through the Holy Spirit. God's mission narrative then continues with a focus on what happens to us. By receiving the Spirit, we become like Christ in his relationship with God (Eph 2:18; Rom 8:14–17; Gal 4:6–7). More specifically, the Spirit unites us with Christ by giving us access to God and God's gifts (Eph 2:18). The Spirit connects us to Christ—through witnessing to Christ (John 15:26; 16:13–4), becoming the person in whom we see and confess Christ (1 Cor 12:3), making Christ present within us (1 John 3:24), and adapting us to the mind and lifestyle of Christ (1 Cor 2:10–16). In this way, our relationship with God is built. Empowered by the Spirit, we can now pray to God (Gal 4:6–7; Rom 8:14–17) and participate in God's mission in imitating the life of Christ (Rom 7:4–6; 2 Cor 5: 17–18). By being bound to Christ by his Spirit, we obtain God's favor and become recipients of God's gifts like Christ; we become like him.[46]

Tanner describes the relationship of the Trinitarian God in two movements. The first movement is by the Word and Spirit as a mission of God for us. The second movement is the achievement of that mission in its influence on us, namely, the movement that allows us to go to God because it is supported by the Word and Spirit. These two movements are cycles that begin and end with God. God started the movement, namely the downward movement by sending the Word and Spirit to complete his mission. In completing it, there is an upward movement, namely a movement back to God, which brings humans along with them.[47]

The movement of God down to us as formed in the mission of Christ's own life is God > Spirit > Jesus (God sent Jesus on a mission through the Spirit, who was the active mediator of Jesus's mission)—like God > Jesus > Spirit (God sent Jesus Christ to us together with the Spirit). In this interrelated way, the transformative effect is on us, understood as an upward movement back to God, when the Spirit makes us children oriented toward God in prayer and service, following the pattern of Spirit > Jesus > God; as individuals Jesus gave us the Spirit, thereby sanctifying us, dedicating us to God's mission of love, following the pattern of Jesus > Spirit > God.[48]

The concept of the relationship of the Trinitarian God can be the theological basis of evangelism. The relationship between Jesus and God is not that of master and subordinate (or slave) but rather a relationship of perfect friendship or partnership when the will of one is naturally aligned with that of the other. In this relationship, there is obedience that follows perfect fellowship (John 15:15). When our humanity is one day completely reworked into the image of Jesus, this is what we will enjoy too: in heaven no command will be heard except the voice of one's own heart.[49]

The Christian experience of evangelism can take the form of a Trinitarian relationship. The work of evangelism is the work of God in Christ with the power of the Holy Spirit to embrace us in this work so that we can join the Trinitarian God in Christ with the power of the Holy Spirit. Meanwhile, the formula for Christian life is that by evangelizing we seek,

---

46. Tanner, *Christ the Key*, 159–60.
47. Tanner, *Christ the Key*, 161.
48. Tanner, *Christ the Key*, 172.
49. Tanner, *Christ the Key*, 172.

discover, and carry out God's will in the world in Jesus Christ with the guidance and power of the Holy Spirit.

There are two successive movements of evangelization as God's mission with different directions. These two movements are distinguished by their respective goals: movement toward God in evangelism as part of worship, and movement toward the world in evangelism as service to God.[50]

The movement of evangelism as a mission is seen in worship as a model of the relationship between God and the world. At the end of worship, there is a blessing, and then we are sent like Christ into the world to do God's work in the power of the Spirit.

Evangelism is a God-directed action, an important dimension of the task given to us on behalf of the world. In serving God through evangelization in the world, we surrender ourselves to a God of love. Our entire life, including worship of God and service to others, in this way becomes an offering to God, a form of God-directed service (see Rom 12:1). The two coincide for the reason that Jesus Christ was human. Jesus Christ is God's worshiper and worker. Both prayer and the work of Jesus's life were offered to God. In God's mission, Jesus Christ and the Holy Spirit returned to God in fulfilled power.

The theological basis of the concept of the Trinitarian God can be a guide to the relational character of evangelism based on a postcolonial feminist missiological perspective. First, the Trinitarian relationship model emphasizes justice and equality between men and women. In evangelization, this relationship must avoid patterns that position women as only "complements" to men.[51] One of the female missionaries sent by RMG to Nias, named Sonia Parera-Hummel, said, "I went to Nias because Uwe [Parera's husband] was sent by UEM to Nias. I was of course interested in going to Nias because this was a part of Indonesia that I didn't know at that time."[52] However, Parera's work in the mission field in Nias can no longer be characterized as merely "complementary" to her husband's work. There are many things she has done for the Nias community from February 1995 to June 2001, including serving as a teacher at the Teacher Preacher School, lecturer at BNKP Sundermann Seminary in Nias, and principal of BNKP Hanna Blindow Kindergarten; delivering lectures; and also preaching at

---

50. Tanner, *Christ the Key*, 161.

51. Adeney, "From the Inside Out," 174.

52. This paragraph draws on my interview with Sonia Parera-Hummel, Sept. 30, 2020.

local congregations. Parera was once chair of the BNKP scholarship to support the BNKP Education Foundation. Apart from that, Parera was also the first head of the library at BNKP Sundermann Seminary. She also formed an informal forum called "Eunike," which is a gathering place for all women priests, not only from BNKP but also from Angowuloa Masehi Indonesia Nias, Orahua Niha Keriso Protestan, and others. For young people, Parera formed "Pniel Singers," a youth choir group with more than forty members in Gunungsitoli. She also holds English-language services at her home once every two weeks and also during church holidays such as Christmas or Easter. The work of missionary women like Parera is real work that does not deserve to be labeled as merely "complementary" to their husbands' work.

Second, the Trinitarian relationships model is not trapped in unhealthy competition and bringing each other down. Postcolonial feminists aim to strengthen each other among women so that together they have intellectual, social, and financial capital so that they can produce change or transformation. Dorothea Richter, one of the women missionary successors of Hanna Blindow, once wrote about her concern about the competition between female missionaries in Protestant and Catholic missions in Nias. However, Richter's confession in her letter is very interesting, and she hopes that there will be no competition in mission work, especially among women. She wrote:

> We have not yet seen the counter-work of Catholic nuns in detail. So we heard that there are four people in charge of kindergarten work, and others will be involved in courses and boarding school work. This will probably result in work similar to ours. It is my daily request that we not allow ourselves to be drawn into competitive struggle, but continue to work joyfully and calmly and trust in God's promises.[53]

Third, the Trinitarian relationships model criticizes "white privilege" in decision-making regarding social transformation for local communities. BNKP currently still has membership relationships with missionary-sending institutions in the past, such as UEM. Apart from that, BNKP also partners with several other international institutions, such as the Lutheran Church of Australia and Kerk in Actie in the Netherlands. These institutions have a vision and mission that is promoted and embodied through the realization of several programs that are under the vision and mission of the institution. On the one hand, this condition illustrates the existence of

---

53. Richter, "Letter to Rheinische Missionsgesellschaft" (Jan. 7, 1961), para. 6.

good and continuous relations between the church and international institutions as a form of ecumenism. On the other hand, existing relationship patterns often lead to the perpetuation of an unequal partnership between the "giver" and the "recipient," especially in finance. Member or partner churches receive financial support from these institutions to the extent that the proposed programs align with their vision and mission. International institutions that are still controlled by Western countries show leadership with "white privilege" to make decisions about what is best for local communities. On the other hand, long-standing dependence on donors has made local churches less able to determine their needs and often trapped, with no choice but to follow the wishes of donors. In the long term, this leadership model does not contribute to the independence of local churches.

Fourth, relationships that emphasize friendship enable mobilization and opportunities for women to lead in high-level and decisive positions in the church.[54] Therefore, postcolonial feminist leadership embraces several feminist leadership values, including encouraging participation, sharing power and information, creating networks, enhancing the self-worth of others, and also energizing others. Leadership aggregates such as the ability to consider, transform, participate, socially express themselves, and orientate in humanity are also strengths for feminist leadership.[55] Some other essential strengths that need to be learned and continuously honed are communication skills (listening well and empathy), mediation skills (conflict resolution), and soft skills in dealing with others.

The characters of a just and equal relationship originate from a theological basis in the concept of the Trinitarian God. Each person in the Trinitarian God is a different person from one another but also inseparable and unmixed. Each person in the Trinitarian God also has the same mission for good for the world but in different ways. In the relationship among the Trinitarian God, no person or role is lower than another because all come from the same God and have the same goal, namely the glory of God and the good of the world. Likewise in evangelistic works: if we view that this work of evangelization belongs to God, then anyone who takes part in it, both men and women, gets the same opportunities and rewards.

I conceptualize evangelism as witnessing to the Trinitarian God through testimonies that give and share life in fair and equal friendly relations in cross-border spaces, especially for voices that have been

---

54. Hertig, "Without a Face," 188.
55. Appelbaum et al., "Gender and Leadership."

marginalized to participate in the invitation to *missio Dei*. Evangelism is part of the *missio Trinitatis*, which gives respect to the local context. Mission belongs to the Trinitarian God, who also invites humans to witness love for others who are different without being limited by nationality, race, class, sex, or gender.

MARTYRDOM AS FRIENDSHIP: A FORM OF CHRISTIAN VIRTUE

The concept of martyrdom has developed over the centuries in the history of religions and philosophy. Various concepts of martyrdom can be found in many faiths. Martyrdom has been a common legacy in settled societies in the Eastern and Mediterranean worlds.[56] I specifically offer the concept of martyrdom as a form of Christian virtue. The meaning of martyrdom has been narrowly understood as people's willingness to die to defend their beliefs. I offer a construction of the concept of martyrdom in evangelization as friendship.

The concept of martyrdom began with the fusion of various ancient philosophical schools, especially stoicism. Philosophers manifest the superiority of wisdom over feelings, and their superiority over a corrupt world by ending their lives or helping others to do so. Philosophers and saints toward the end of the Roman Empire chose martyrdom, the practice of dramatic death, as a symbol of opposition to unjust authority.

The practice of martyrdom is also adopted by monotheistic religions. If someone expresses different beliefs and views bravely, then the logical consequence is to become a victim who is called a martyr (Greek: *martus*). However, the three monotheistic religions—Judaism, Christianity, and Islam—connect the term "martyr" with another concept, namely confession or testimony, so this meaning creates a new and wider semantic field. *Martyrdom* is people's willingness to surrender their life to God. This concept exists in all three religions. In Christianity, martyrdom is synonymous with the principle "Your cruelty is my glory." This principle is different than the Jewish understanding, namely "sanctifying in the name of God," and also than Islam, namely "dying for God."[57]

During the early centuries of Christianity, martyrdom was a known constant during an era called the "age of the martyrs." The figure that is

---

56. Hatina, *Martyrdom in Modern Islam*, 19.
57. Hatina, *Martyrdom in Modern Islam*, 26.

the model for martyrdom is Jesus Christ, namely the sacrificial lamb who atones for human sins. Jesus's willingness to passively endure death became a model for persecuted believers during the Roman Empire during the first three hundred years of the first millennium. Martyrs in early Christian history died passively at the hands of kidnappers and oppressors. This death is different than death that is self-inflicted as a choice.

Meir Hatina explores the concept of martyrdom in Christianity, which he connects with the views of historical figures and events that helped popularize this concept in his time. Hatina traces Tertullian of Carthage's understanding of martyrdom, which was highly developed in the early days of Christianity. Tertullian had a martyr's motto that he once expressed to a Roman governor, namely, "Your persecution is our glory."[58] Tertullian emphasized that the Christian's calling is to suffer to achieve victory. Victory is not the result of defeating the enemy on the battlefield but rather holding fast to one's beliefs even though one has to face the enemy's cruelty. For Tertullian, being a martyr was an ethical exercise in obeying God's will. God's will tests the endurance of Christian faith and loyalty in persecution and execution. Satan is not a rival of Christianity, but he is an agent of God by whom Christian loyalty is tested. On the opposite side, Jesus and the Holy Spirit are heavenly messengers who help Christians remain faithful.

The martyr is resistant to pain because he is strengthened by the name of Jesus, who has risen to overcome physical weakness and give encouragement in persecution. Moreover, the martyr is the personification of the church in the microcosmos. This identification goes hand in hand with another statement from Tertullian that "the blood of martyrs is the seed of the church."[59] Tertullian's views influenced many Christians to be ready to become martyrs during the Roman Empire. Eternal salvation was valued more highly than physical survival, so Christian martyrs were prepared to undergo torture. The influence on the expansion of Christianity was that the higher the number of martyrs, the wider the public's memory of and sympathy for them.

The tradition of martyrdom is also strengthened by several other factors such as literature or narratives of martyrs, grave visits, and liturgy to commemorate the martyrs. Martyr literature (Latin: *acta martyrum*) became the most popular literary genre during the period of the formation

---

58. Hatina, *Martyrdom in Modern Islam*, 26.
59. Hatina, *Martyrdom in Modern Islam*, 27.

of the church.[60] Churches and graves of martyrs have become pilgrimage destinations. Touching graves or participating in evening prayers at monasteries to restore health or induce holy visions was widespread. Another practice that reflects the strong tradition of martyrdom is the desire of believers to be buried close to the martyr's grave so that they will be resurrected to live with the martyr. In addition, there are also memorial festivals and public processions in memory of a martyr that end at ritual sites associated with the martyr. It is not only the martyrs who receive honor but also their families. Would-be martyrs who survived the torture and lived on were also ultimately given prestigious positions and high status within the church.

Martyrdom is also seen as a "second baptism" because the blood of martyrs promises cleansing from all sins and entry into heaven. Self-sacrifice is a very important act in Christianity. The suffering of martyrdom served a high purpose. In Christianity, suffering expresses infinite love, compassion, and atonement for the sins of humanity tied to self-sacrifice, as demonstrated by Jesus on the cross. In essence, early Christian martyrdom was a passive protest against the use of violence and challenged the oppressive power structure. In addition, there is a principle in martyrdom that there is an authority higher than human authority. Although some Christians had served as Roman soldiers, they refused to use violence to protect themselves. The execution of Christians increased their number of admirers.[61]

A large number of martyrs in early Christianity were women. They played subordinate roles but were still heroic. Their achievements were felt and also helped raise the status of their male colleagues. Women subjected to cruel treatment by courts and condemned to execution received attention and empathy. In particular, the phenomenon of early Christian martyrdom occurred in urban areas of the Roman Empire. The location of the martyr's death was in the prison and the central square, so a large crowd of spectators publicized it and caused discussion in the wider community. During the first and second centuries AD, acts of martyrdom provided an opportunity for nonbelievers to choose to become Christians. The eagerness of the early Christians to die at the hands of their oppressors attracted the attention of nonbelievers.

---

60. Hatina, *Martyrdom in Modern Islam*, 27.
61. Hatina, *Martyrdom in Modern Islam*, 27.

The spirit of martyrdom in early Christians also gave rise to disagreements in early Christian theology. Although the martyr's redemption and passage to heaven were always seen as certain, the specific quest for spiritual security in this way was not always supported by the church. The reason is that true martyrdom must result from God's will, not human will. This dispute was initiated by Clement of Alexandria, who argued that etymologically martyrdom means "bearing testimony," that is, a confession of faith in God. Everyone who believes in God and obeys God's laws is a martyr, both in word and deed. Such martyrdom does not always require death. In addition, for Clement, forced martyrdom by Rome was only one form of martyrdom, but even that was not the optimal way to become a martyr. Testimony can be achieved by professing faith in a much more optimistic way.[62]

Martyrdom rituals remained an important component of Christian religious life through the second half of the fourth century. Preaching about the martyrs is a primary means of recontextualization into the present and future. Historical accuracy is not the primary interest in listening to the sermon but rather adherence to the beliefs and the act of sacrifice itself. This historical core is mixed with hagiography that seeks to present the martyr as a holy human being, whose behavior embodied the highest Christian virtues. History was transformed into a hagiography decorated with stylistic elements and quotations from sacred texts.

The blood of the martyrs became the seed of the church, as Tertullian said, describing how the seed was planted, watered, and nourished by those who supported the pedagogical system. It is not surprising, then, that Roman Catholics developed a certified martyrology, a well-organized list of martyrs with birth dates and brief biographies, i.e., a kind of martyrological lexicon. It is an awareness of the blood ties between today's Christians and those who suffered and gave their lives for the holy kingdom that is officially maintained.

Written and unwritten testimonies in the traditions of hagiography, liturgy, sermons, poetry, drama, paintings, statues, and letters strengthen the memory of the martyrs. Likewise, the body and clothing relics of the martyrs are miracles that need to be preserved. There was an encouragement of hagiographic discourse and elaboration of constructed graves of martyrs from the second century onwards. The graves of the martyrs were seen as public property and accessible to everyone and were the focus

---

62. Hatina, *Martyrdom in Modern Islam*, 29.

of rituals attended by the entire community. Records of martyrs become larger than life, while grains of authentic historical information about them shrink or disappear.

There are several purposes to the narrative of these martyrs. The first goal is to turn the martyrs into a living memory, thereby encouraging believers to follow in their footsteps. The second goal is to build a Christian identity. Martyrdom is a manifestation of Christian virtues that are worth cultivating. In addition, the hagiography is shaped by the congregation itself, thus contributing to a blend of congregational identity, theological themes, or laws to which congregation members adhere. At the same time, martyrdom gives Christians ammunition in case of disagreement in their relations with other religions or with other sects within Christianity itself. Sometimes, one Christian group justifies its persecution of a rival group by claiming that the rival martyrs were not true martyrs but simply desperate fanatics who committed suicide by sacrificing themselves to their enemies. Apart from that, two basics of martyrdom testimony are traditionally understood, namely steadfastness of faith and the ability to endure pain steadfastly. These two things continued to shape Christian thought, which was later developed into the realm of asceticism. The sanctity of martyrs is also attributed to those who spread the gospel or who led the church in a spirit of ascesis.

There are different concepts of martyrdom narratives between early Christian history and the concept of martyrdom that emerged in Christianity during the Crusades in the eleventh century. At that time, the murdered Crusaders began to be seen as martyrs because the church promised that their sins would be forgiven. The Crusades are thus an important episode in the history of martyrdom. These wars also introduced in Western Europe the idea of a new path to martyrdom, namely death in the struggle against pagans for the sake of Jesus and His community. However, the idea of martyrdom penetrated the consciousness of the Crusaders only gradually. The term "martyr" was not used, although promises of a place with the saints and heavenly salvation were made to those who died in the Crusades. The initial definition of martyrdom was to fight and die for a holy cause, but the church's first steps were still hesitant. However, there is no clear promise by the church regarding martyr status. Moreover, certain circles criticized the Crusaders because they were motivated by commercial interests or worldly glory.

The large number of published editions of books on martyrs seems to indicate that Christian martyrdom was a popular aspect of the culture of the Crusades period. All Christian denominations celebrate their heroism, creating a tradition of martyrdom that becomes part of the collective identity. Martyrdom also created dissonance, even separate identities, when Christians from different denominations lived as good neighbors. In addition to depicting the executions of martyrs, books of martyrs include letters written from prison, poetry, and statements of faith. These materials are edited to improve their quality and increase their universal appeal. A survey of the letters shows that the martyrs' narratives reflect not only personal feelings but also an opportunity to urge their peers and readers, in general, to show fidelity to the faith and sacrifices they lived joyfully. Their sermons were expressed in scriptural terminology imbued with religious fervor to legitimize and promote their views and personal coping skills. They put their trust in God and Jesus as the goal of their martyrdom.

Apart from the background of the meaning of martyrdom in the history of the church in the past, nowadays martyrdom also has developmental meaning. Bryan Stone understands "martyrdom" as the primary virtue of ecclesiological evangelization. *Martyria*, for Stone, has nothing to do with the glorification of suffering, let alone suffering as redemption. Rather, martyrdom is a costly public testimony to Christ's lordship over power that is enabled and fostered by the church as a "disciplined community of virtue."[63] Stone selects and discusses martyrdom within the framework of the presence of virtue, patience, courage, and humility as things that are very important for a faithful evangelistic witness today.

Lakawa also gives a new meaning to martyrdom. She connects the missionary image with the theory of martyrdom, especially when it comes to witnesses.[64] According to Lakawa, mission and martyrdom are two interrelated topics. The question now is whether this martyrdom theory is adequate in the current context when it comes to evangelism.

Lakawa offers a different meaning of martyrdom. First, the essence of martyrdom is rooted in the experience of death in faith but is more ingrained in the experience of living in faith. Martyrdom is not only about the dead but also about life, that is, about living life in faithful witness to the life of Jesus. The deaths of martyrs are the deaths of people who fought to the death to defend their Christian faith. The martyrs are seen to have

---

63. Stone, *Evangelism after Christendom*, 163.
64. Lakawa, "Missiologi Luka," 23.

died like Jesus, so now, using the deaths of the martyrs as a reference for their faith, believers strive to live like Jesus. Martyrdom is about witnessing a life of "faithfully following Jesus" and "becoming like" Jesus. Martyrdom is a life that bears witness to the life and ministry of Jesus, namely a life that brings justice and hope to the marginalized. This way of life bears witness to the death and resurrection of Jesus, which makes life a promise of life for those who fight for justice. The concept of martyrdom is reconfigured in the Christian practice of witnessing. Martyrdom is reappropriated through the call to "remember" Jesus.[65]

Second, martyrdom requires new practices that embed the concept of martyrdom in everyday life.[66] Stories of martyrdom reconnect the past and weave new possibilities for continuing how to be witnesses of a living God who gives hope to those who carry them on. Martyrs are those who "lived to tell the story," whose testimony is "a discourse of survival for hope and hope for survival."[67] This dimension of martyrdom is related to faith and justice that are projected in experience.

Continuing the thoughts of Stone and Lakawa, I offer the concept of martyrdom in evangelization based on the framework of friendly love. John 15:13 says, "No one has greater love than this, to lay down one's life for one's friends." The giving of life is not a glorification of death; on the contrary, it is, rather, a glorification of life. Evangelism as witnessing to God is the story of how God gives and maintains life with the love of a friend who is willing to sacrifice and share life with others.

In the history of ecumenical missions, Dana Robert found a historical recording of the International Mission Conference in 1910. The recording was a speech by a participant named V. S. Azariah. As was described earlier, Azariah's speech was a criticism of the European mission movement at a time when most of Asia and Africa were still European colonies. Azariah emphasized, "Too often you promise us thrones in heaven, but will not offer us chairs in your drawing rooms."[68] What Azariah wanted was a friendly relationship that became the basis of evangelism and mission. More than that, his words are a call to friendship on a mission that transcends race, class, and culture. This kind of friendship is enlivened by missionaries who

---

65. Lakawa, "Risky Hospitality," 246.
66. Lakawa, "Risky Hospitality," 247.
67. Lakawa, "Risky Hospitality," 247.
68. Robert, "From 'Give Us Friends,'" 198.

have traveled far from their home countries and sacrificed their lives for the conversion of others.

Robert appreciates Azariah's thoughts from a postcolonial perspective. Azariah's observations marked a milestone in the history of the development of international relations. They claim a shared vision of a transnational, interracial, and multicultural Christian community. Within this common framework, he challenged the 1910 Edinburgh delegates to live the values of the reign of God. This vision included equality among people of all races, united through what he called "spiritual friendship" in Jesus Christ.[69]

Postcolonial readings challenge the binary view between the racist, romantic West and the non-West. The postcolonial perspective opens up a new interpretative space for martyrdom as a basis for the evangelization of friendship that allows a space for "hybridity" to develop. Martyrdom is life-giving, which opens the boundaries of nationality, race, sex, gender, and social class so that there is a longing to give and receive each other in friendly relations. The postcolonial approach allows the formation of space for friendship and cooperation that reflects respect for different identities.

Azariah's speech reveals that Christ's witness does not involve condemnation or coercion but is rooted in reciprocal relationships with people who are different. Missions should embrace friendship as an authentic missionary practice. The mission itself is a significant space in which cross-cultural relationships can be built and developed. While friendship does not necessarily resolve oppression or remedy structural racism or colonialism, it certainly testifies against oppressive relations.

Martyrdom as friendship in missions can be discovered through the documented narratives of the personal experiences of missionaries. These documents, which are often viewed as minor narratives, have become powerful sources for the development of cross-cultural, transnational, and cross-border missions. Robert realized that the difficulty of researching existing sources was the long-standing neglect of the impact of friendship on missions.[70] Therefore, a postcolonial perspective is useful for resurrecting narratives of friendship that have been hidden under formal theological language such as cooperation, fellowship, internationalism, ecumenism, brotherhood, partnership, and the reign of God. Resurrecting such narratives requires searching for and uncovering narratives that go beyond

---

69. Robert, "From 'Give Us Friends,'" 197.
70. Robert, "From 'Give Us Friends,'" 214.

conference reports and formal correspondence. These friendship narratives can be found in diaries, autobiographies, and other more personal sources and reveal stories of transoceanic friendship that live in oral memory.

In the concept of evangelism, martyrdom as friendship is a gift given to someone whose life is a testimony to the Trinity of God for their friends. Terry Muck and Frances Adeney understand mission as a gift narrative. The Christian's responsibility is to witness to what God has done in Jesus Christ, who has offered salvation as a gift. Muck and Adeney argue that gift giving is a mission metaphor, which means that we are more than conquerors of nations, more than reapers of souls, and more than winners of metaphysical arguments, but we are bearers of gifts. The greatest gift is the story of what God has done for the world through Jesus Christ to his friends.[71]

Evangelism as a Christian mission in history is seen from the lens of martyrdom, namely the gift giving of a friend who has shared life through health, education, and community building based on the gift of grace from Jesus Christ. Thus, martyrdom as friendship is a commitment to the kingdom of God that continually gives oneself to others and is also open to offers of cross-cultural, cross-racial, and other cross-border friendships.

In Nias society, the practice of gift giving is known to strengthen relationships. The term "gift giving" in the Nias language is known as giving *böwö*. The meaning of *böwö* is very rich and connected to the concept of hospitality. Although in marriage relations the concept of *böwö* is often reduced in meaning to bride-price, I offer a reexamination of the meaning of this term so that it is not relegated to just a transactional relationship or mere domestic hospitality.[72] *Böwö* was not limited to bride-price but rather a virtue that prioritized hospitality as a core value of Nias culture. *Böwö* is a form of complementarity between communities by participating in each other's lives to create unity. Participation in a "give-and-receive" relationship means starting a symbiotic and reciprocal relationship as a shared commitment in society. *Böwö* as hospitality is a lifestyle of the Nias people. *Böwö* accommodates space for reciprocal relationships, respecting each other's rules and upholding each other's commitments.

The concept of martyrdom as friendship and the concept of *böwö* as hospitality can become the basis for evangelization that is no longer based on hierarchical, patriarchal, and transactional relationships. Martyrdom fosters various relationships in evangelization as part of the commitment

---

71. Muck and Adeney, *Christianity Encountering World Religion*.
72. Harefa, "*Böwö*."

and maintenance of embedded Christian values, specifically the value of love. The concept of *böwö* allows hospitality to be celebrated in long-term friendly relationships. *Böwö* is not based on transactions but on love. The love that exists is celebrated in the joy of being a martyr, namely being a friend who is willing to give life and also accept the life shared by people who are different.

In the end, I argue a postcolonial feminist missiological perspective provides a strong basis for criticizing and deconstructing concepts of evangelism that are still patriarchal and colonial as found in documents, materials, and narratives of evangelism and mission at BNKP. This chapter has also offered reconstruction in three special parts, namely the biblical narrative of evangelism in the Gospel of Matthew, the concept of the Trinitarian God as a model for postcolonial mission communities, and martyrdom as friendship.

CONCLUSION

Evangelism as a mission based on a postcolonial approach challenges the theological and practical sources of the church, which are still confined by patriarchal domination and the legacy of colonialism in the past. These theological sources come from the church's theological concept of who God is and God's relationship with humans through *missio Dei*. Therefore, there is a need for a postcolonial reconstruction of evangelism that includes the theological-ecclesial-missiological implications of the historical narrative of evangelism for the status, role, and contribution of women in evangelism today.

The narrative of the Gospel of Matthew from a postcolonial perspective is the narrative of a marginalized community seeking to challenge the hierarchical domination of a tyrant ruler. Matthew 28, especially vv. 18–20, is often an instrument to legitimize evangelism. Not infrequently, these verses are also used for domination over others, including the domination of men over women. Therefore, awareness of this layer of power can be found through recognizing the context of Matthew in his time and how the Gospel of Matthew also speaks to the current generation of people.

Theologically, the concept of the Trinitarian God as the basis for evangelism also requires reconstruction. I offer the Trinitarian community as a model of a postcolonial mission community. The issue of unequal power relations due to colonialism and patriarchy in the past has colored the history of evangelism as a mission. So, a theological basis for evangelism is needed that supports the ideas of justice and equality in differences. In Christianity, the source of this theology can be found through the concept of the Trinitarian God. Interpersonal relationships in the communion of God the Trinity are relationships that depend on each other and do not exclude each other. Each person in the Trinity operates differently in the same and inseparable mission. Likewise, the relationship between each person involved and participating in God's mission is not to dominate each other and marginalize others, especially women. Evangelism as a mission activity that witnesses the work of the Trinitarian God in just and equal relationships is in direct conflict with the motivations of domination, manipulation, and violence to dominate others.

Another theological resource in Christianity related to evangelism and missions is martyrdom. I offer the concept of martyrdom as friendship, namely a form of Christian virtue. Women have played a significant role in God's missionary work in the world. Many of them have also become martyrs in a holistic sense, namely martyrdom that is focused not only on death but especially on sharing life by living Christ as a testimony to others. Martyrdom like this has been largely forgotten and also distorted by limited meaning. Therefore, space for appreciation is needed for women who have played a role in evangelization and missions, one of which is through their biographical narratives as living witnesses of God's work.

5

A RECONSTRUCTION OF EVANGELISM FROM A POSTCOLONIAL FEMINIST MISSIOLOGICAL PERSPECTIVE

STORY THEOLOGY AS EMBODIED STORY WITH PRISM READING

THERE IS POWER IN stories. Choan-Seng Song saw this power as unique to Asia and initiated story theology as a source of theology. Stories contain cultural and spiritual depth about human experiences regarding the mysteries of life, anxiety, injustice, oppression, and liberation. Stories about despair and hope, doubt, and faith, as well as the search for moral strength, enable humans to survive in a world twisted by evil and oppressive powers.[1] Folk tales are parables about human life in which we can find simple but profound story theology.[2]

When conveying God's message, Jesus used stories so that the listeners could easily understand. Jesus got these stories from the environment that raised him. Jesus was good at telling stories. The stories he tells contain God's message about love, justice, peace, forgiveness, and hope while suffering. What is interesting is that the story of Jesus's life is also a story that God uses to save many people. The story of Jesus's life, suffering, death, and resurrection is God's message to humans about justice and God's love for

---

1. Song, *Sebutkanlah Nama-Nama Kami*, 15.
2. Song, *Sebutkanlah Nama-Nama Kami*, 15.

the world. For more than two thousand years, the story of Jesus's life has been a story that inspires and saves humanity from the hopelessness and destruction of life. This is where the power of stories, narratives, or tales lies, namely when these stories become a source of life for those who are oppressed.

For Song, local stories are very rich in meaning and are a source of local theology. Song tells several local stories connected to life values, such as the power of giving names, issues of love facing the search for justice, human stupidity, and repentance, to stories about ethics and politics, which he interprets theologically. Not all stories can be a source of theology in evangelism. The story is not just any event or idea but rather the gift of the gospel in the form of an embodied story that testifies to the Trinitarian God and God's work in the world, especially for those who are marginalized.

The theological basis of the embodied story is "the messenger becomes the message." Kosuke Koyama argues that a person who is sent to convey God's message can only be a living person. Thus, the message and the messenger must become one.[3] Koyama argues that if the news conveyed is in persons, in the life of the messengers, then the news through their lives is conveyed.[4] The news becomes embodied news. In the event of Jesus Christ, Koyama argues that through the bodily message "the one who conveys the message" is more important than "what is conveyed."[5] The messenger not only carries the message, but the message has become a part of him.

The position of the herald remains as God's messenger to convey God's message. It was God who made them messengers because God gave them this task. The anchor is not ready-made but is formed in a continuous process towards full involvement. The messengers must realize that they are involved by God in God's mission.

Koyama also explains how someone can become a messenger of God as a bearer of the gospel. First, a messenger must live in awareness of human life and he/she is sent into a complicated and complex historical life. His/her call came from God, who loves humanity. Second, a messenger can do his/her job. This ability continues to be honed in active involvement in the apostolic life through a process that requires fortitude and patience. Third, a messenger continues to direct his/her thoughts toward "the unity of the message with the bearer of the Gospel." Of course, no human being

---

3. Kosuke Koyama, *Injil dalam Pandangan Asia*, 272.
4. Koyama, *Injil dalam Pandangan Asia*, 273.
5. Koyama, *Injil dalam Pandangan Asia*, 273.

can fully achieve this unity, but this also does not mean that humans cannot progress towards it.[6]

Based on Koyama's views, I offer the life stories of women missionaries who witness God through the testimony of their words and deeds as embodied stories. This theological basis becomes the basis for evangelism as storytelling.

Song uses a cultural lens in his approach when building story theology. However, Song does not pay specific attention to women's struggles and how these local stories have an impact on women's real and everyday life experiences. The main question in story theology is whether this theology can answer the struggles of women's lives, especially the experience of injustice and oppression of patriarchal culture which is intertwined with the power of colonialism. Another question is: What form would these stories take if told by women? The story theology promoted by Song has provided a strong basis for the significance of narrative in the development of folk theology, but it still does not answer the need for women's liberation from the entanglement of domination they experience.

When hearing stories told from generation to generation, women generally compare them with their experiences and stories of their lives in the entanglement of various dominations. When women then retell the story, it opens up the possibility of paying attention or criticizing parts that are not paid attention to by male speakers, who have different life experiences from women. In addition, an emphasis on the Asian context alone can reinforce the binary understanding of East and West or Asia and Europe, making it difficult to see the vision of cooperation in evangelism as a multidirectional narrative of friendship.

The story theology initiated by Song needs to be criticized and enriched from a postcolonial feminist perspective. In his writing, Song uses an open approach to feminine symbols such as a merciful God, specifically in the story of Jesus, who is merciful (Matt 9:36).[7] However, Song uses Asian stories from the perspective and experience of being a man. Apart from that, Song's narrative approach does not offer systematic-constructive theological thinking that can simply be applied in developing a constructive missiology with a feminist postcolonial perspective.

To enrich the story theology initiated by Song, I use Musa Dube's thoughts as a constructive basis. Dube offers a method of reading stories

---

6. Koyama, *Injil dalam Pandangan Asia*, 278–81.
7. Song, *Sebutkanlah Nama-Nama Kami*, 15.

called "prism reading" to analyze ancient literature, local narratives, and especially biblical narratives.[8] Prism reading is a way of reading with postcolonial feminist eyes from many angles by seeing, reading, and hearing texts to resist colonial and patriarchal oppressive structures and ideologies. The prism reading serves to remind readers that patriarchy and oppression in various forms and levels are experienced by women in different ways in each culture. This reading touches on the discourse of colonization and precolonial patriarchy. In addition, this method encourages sensitivity to the issue of historical oppression by existing powers. These forms of domination overlap and are intertwined but are not identical. Women from different cultures may be able to talk about different forms of patriarchy and colonization, but not all of them experience double colonization. Prism reading can help to understand the tension between colonizers and colonized through literature or texts as inherent in a world that has been damaged by various forms and levels of imperial and patriarchal oppression. This means that feminist readers and writers cannot avoid the parameters of colonial and decolonization practices to move toward liberation movements.

The prism reading offered by Dube has several characteristics. First, prism reading allows for political coalitions that go beyond the interests of certain identities. In one space and time, a person can be the subject of many feminist negotiations such as differences in class, race, culture, religion, nation, ethnicity, sexuality, and the world.[9]

Second, prism reading does not aim to create a "parrot portrait," that is, when the readers just follow what the text tells them to do. Prism reading is a reading that resists destructive power and witnesses awakening. This reading provides space for the body to speak and talk from their own heart and mind. Prism reading subverts genres and language that have been dominated by retelling history. This reading also builds radical decolonization through a hybrid narrative that refuses to privilege precolonial patriarchy that was culturally, economically, and politically oppressive.[10]

Third, prism reading emphasizes the experience of awakening from the oppression of the authorities and analyzes its narrative representation but also refuses to limit itself to these texts. Although there is room to build a radical hybrid decolonization discourse, this reading does not limit itself

---

8. Dube, *Postcolonial Feminist Interpretation*, 121.
9. Dube, *Postcolonial Feminist Interpretation*, 122.
10. Dube, *Postcolonial Feminist Interpretation*, 122.

to this. In contrast, prism reading diligently cultivates postcolonial spaces to spin new authentic narratives that fight for equality, difference, and liberation.[11]

Fourth, prism reading challenges boldly and responsibly to begin to utilize new postcolonial feminist spaces without being satisfied with reforming structures built on unequal foundations and oppressive foundations. This reading aims to revolutionize structural oppression by cultivating reading-writing that provides space for interdependence and mutual liberation when differences, equality and justice for various cultures, religions, genders, classes, sexualities, ethnicities, and races can be celebrated.[12]

BIOGRAPHY AS THEOLOGY, EVANGELISM AS EMBODIED STORY

James Wm. McClendon Jr. understands that the power of a biography is that the images found in the life of the figures narrated can speak and convey messages to the reader.[13] These figures have a special character that makes them known and understood. They have the ability to face critical situations in their lives and to achieve their goals. The figures narrated are persons who have a vision in their lives. Living a life guided by a strong vision is one of the best ways to understand one's "religious experience," which can later become a source for theology.

There are two arguments offered by McClendon regarding biography as theology. First, biography as theology is intended not only for the benefit of the individual concerned but for the community that has inherited the Christian tradition and also a life based on God's word.[14] The subject in a biography as theology is a figure who has contributed to the theology of a community of believers primarily by showing how certain archetypal images of that faith apply to the life and circumstances of that community. The Bible is certainly the "focus" for understanding the narrative of this figure's life because through it we can understand the central vision of theology, namely the encountering and relationship between God and humans. For example, in the initial narrative of Genesis, the relationship between God and humans is described as Creator and creation so that readers are directed

---

11. Dube, *Postcolonial Feminist Interpretation*, 122.
12. Dube, *Postcolonial Feminist Interpretation*, 123.
13. McClendon, *Biography as Theology*, 90.
14. McClendon, *Biography as Theology*, 91.

to know who they are before God, explore God's nature and character, learn how to relate to each other, and so on.

Second, biography as theology is based on a person's life experience.[15] The experience is the life journey of the figure that brings the message of the gospel as an image of mission and the fulfillment of God's purposes into interactions with humanity.[16] For McClendon, in writing a biography there may be the possibility of bias occurring, for example, that related to expressing feelings, desires, hopes, fears, fantasies, imaginations, longings, or visions. However, biography as theology not only has room to be appreciated and accepted but also evaluated.

Harry Meserve argues that the true-life experiences of religious figures are revealed in their biographies or autobiographies. This biography can be analyzed to discover the early experiences and insights that shaped the figures' characters and beliefs, namely a force that drove definitive actions in their life. Meserve emphasizes that belief is the real strength that is the driving factor in the figures' life. This belief can be found precisely in the figures' actions rather than the formal beliefs that prevail in the church or the school of thought they follow. True belief or faith is revealed in the life lived, namely when the Word becomes flesh.[17]

Most people prefer to read stories rather than theological formulations. This is the appeal of a biography, namely that the reader can reflect on the experiences, insights, and greatness of the figures' souls through their life story. The story also speaks to the readers so that they can understand what it means to experience the figures' experiences. The theological values found in a person's biographical narrative may be more confusing than formal statements. However, these narratives show the human side of a person more and are also more able to convince the reader.[18]

According to Meserve, several things are important in writing a biography as theology. First, large collections of information about the attitudes and behavior of particular figures are an important source for gaining insight into theological values. Basic theological propositions about human nature based on observations of behavioral records can be called "genuine potentialities." Human nature is the raw material from which the figure becomes a civilized, constructive, and loving person. Second, apart from

---

15. McClendon, *Biography as Theology*, 92.
16. McClendon, *Biography as Theology*, 103.
17. Meserve, "Biography as Theology," 230.
18. Meserve, "Biography as Theology," 227.

information about the figures, the forces that work in society are also very important because these forces help shape the figures' process towards growth, development, and personality education.[19] Third is information about their journey to meet the beliefs or myths of each culture. The figures see themselves as a pilgrim moving through a dangerous unknown area, full of threats and promises and the possibility of good and evil. On the one hand, they were respected because of their experiences on the pilgrimage. On the other hand, they are also captivated by other people's experiences. The experience can depict a journey of moving step by step, not knowing what the day might bring but never running away, and reflecting on the journey. When they rest, they may encounter an oasis in the desert or a safe anchorage if they are at sea. The figures may stop to rest on the journey, but they may not stay persistently. So, the travel situation can give an idea of the uncomfortable side of life, and at the same time, there is also a sense of vitality. This is what Meserve calls "pilgrim's progress."[20] Fourth is awareness of death and the value that awareness can add to life. The figures' life story allows readers to view death more honestly and accept it more wisely. By accepting death, a person can find more value and meaning in life.

Biography may not be the most orderly and rational method of studying theology, but it teaches about the art of living, namely the art of learning how to live this life constantly and wisely. Like life itself, biography is often turbulent, confusing, and contradictory, but in fact, it is also sometimes gentle, open, and sublime. Biography adds a human quality to theology, and that is something theology has always needed.

According to Laurence Cantwell, a biography is more than just a curriculum vitae. Biography is a literary form that aims to take the reader inside another human being to communicate with the reader uniquely. Biography is an exploration of someone's mind and heart through which the reader is invited to live another person's life. When readers have read a person's biography, they finally know not only what that figure did but also why they did it. In this way, the reader gets the key to this figure's life by understanding the patterns that explain their inner consistency through their words and actions. Every biography is a failure in the sense that there are always limitations to communicating the incommunicable. Of course, it

---

19. Meserve, "Biography as Theology," 229.
20. Meserve, "Biography as Theology," 230.

is impossible to get a complete narrative of the life of particular figures and record it in a biography.[21]

The question asked by Cantwell is whether the Gospels can be called biographies. Cantwell views this paradoxically. On the one hand, the Bible with all its realism, factual accuracy, clarity of vision, and honesty of narrative can contain biographical elements. On the other hand, the Gospel narrative is not just a biography of Jesus but a biography of the figures who met Jesus. Although the focus of attention is almost constant on Christ, the perspective of the Gospel is always someone else's. The faith of the disciples can be biased, but it does not distort the views that Christ's contemporaries had about him. From the perspective of resurrection faith, the disciples faithfully reported the reactions of themselves and others to the extraordinary reality of the earthly life of Jesus Christ. Mary, John the Baptist, Peter, the Pharisees, sinners, sick people, soldiers, politicians, traitors: all are held up as mirrors so that the readers can see themselves in the mirror.[22]

According to Cantwell, in theory, there is no reason why the Gospels should not be called biographies of Jesus for kerygmatic or catechetical purposes.[23] Biography aims to record the life of a particular figure, remember or reminisce about that figure, and bring it back to life in the reader's heart.

When biography is understood as something more than just a curriculum vitae, people see that the Bible does not fail as a biography, even though the Gospels are at the same time not primarily a biography. The Gospels can be called nonbiographical because, in the Gospel narrative, Jesus is the center of attention, but the story is never written from Jesus's point of view. Nor do the disciples attempt to identify themselves or their readers with the person of Christ. They are witnesses of what Jesus did and report what he said, but they are not the medium that allows us to know what it is like to be Christ. They are not biographers. Readers can describe what Jesus said and did but cannot understand him. Readers can provide a curriculum vitae and convey his words but cannot write his biography. There is a paradox because the Gospels with all their realism have presented the lives of figures who witnessed Jesus Christ, which became an encouragement and memory, and stimulated others to live in faith in him.[24]

21. Cantwell, "Gospels as Biographies," 194.
22. Cantwell, "Gospels as Biographies," 200.
23. Cantwell, "Gospels as Biographies," 193.
24. Cantwell, "Gospels as Biographies," 196.

I connect those previous theories to the rediscovery of women's narratives in evangelism and missions in Nias, Indonesia. Nowadays, Christianity needs evangelism that learns from historical failures when the spirit of patriarchy and colonialism was very dominant. Evangelism is expected to be able to answer today's challenges to achieve liberation, justice, and equality, specifically for women. The church needs an evangelism concept that provides greater space for women to have their voices heard.

When writing about women and missions, Robert in her book *Christian Mission* explains how Christianity became a world religion through storytelling. Robert tells stories about women missionaries such as Annalena Tonelli and Ann Judson. Annalena Tonelli helped sick and poor people in Somalia. She became a mother figure, sister, and friend.[25] Tonelli's life explains the meaning of mission as service.[26] Another missionary woman was Ann Judson, a missionary's wife who served in Burma. During Judson's ministry, a pattern of mission partnerships between men and women began to take shape. Judson adopted orphans, taught girls, translated Bible passages, and wrote the first history of the American mission in Burma.[27]

Robert saw that missionary women had participated in the creation of distinctive mission theories and that they had influenced the shape of the mission and the social transformation of society. Women missionaries are both thinkers and doers of mission movements. Robert explored the history, thoughts, and practices of missions carried out by women. On the one hand, women's thoughts and roles in missions were a liberating step, and on the other hand, they were still limited by gender issues, unclear positions, and a lack of recognition of the transformational movements that have been carried out. Therefore, for Robert, it is important to observe the female missionary figures and also the stereotypes or caricatures attached to them. These stereotypes and caricatures contain the life experiences of missionary women with difficult struggles.[28] Women missionaries also lead tiring, frustrating lives, and unfortunately, their service is considered inferior to that of their husbands or male missionary colleagues.

I offer evangelism as storytelling based on a postcolonial feminist perspective and martyrdom theory. Based on martyrdom theory, storytelling is not just a story that is told but a story that is lived and embodied.

---

25. Robert, *Christian Mission*, 118.
26. Robert, *Christian Mission*, 118.
27. Robert, "Protestant Women Missionaries," 2:836.
28. Robert, *American Women in Mission*, 72.

The women described at the end of this chapter establish the essence of evangelism as a Christian presence. Martyrdom becomes the main virtue of ecclesiological evangelization. Martyrdom is not related to the glorification of death but rather is a public witness within the framework of the presence of Christians who establish virtue, patience, courage, and humility as very important things for friendly evangelistic witness.[29]

The theological basis for evangelism as storytelling also refers to the *TTL* document, which states:

> Mission has been understood as a movement taking place from the center to the periphery, and from the privileged to the marginalized of society. Now people at the margins are claiming their key role as agents of mission and affirming mission as transformation. This reversal of roles in the envisioning of mission has strong biblical foundations because God chose the poor, the foolish, and the powerless (1 Cor. 1:18–31) to further God's mission of justice and peace so that life may flourish. If there is a shift of the mission concept from "mission to the margins" to "mission from the margins," what then is the distinctive contribution of the people from the margins? And why are their experiences and visions crucial for re-imagining mission and evangelism today?[30]

By the telling of women's narratives, which have so far been seen as marginal narratives, the mission can change direction: from a mission to those who are marginalized to a mission by those who are marginalized. The experiences, understanding, roles, and leadership of women in patriarchal societies are often marginalized voices. By having their stories told, marginalized voices gain space for recognition and appreciation.

There are three characteristics or dimensions of evangelism as storytelling. First, it is a testimony to the Trinitarian God and God's work through specific and significant narratives, voices, roles, experiences, and understandings of women in evangelism. These stories are the gospel that has been lived by women whose beliefs give rise to hope for survival, liberation from oppression, and strengthening solidarity among women. The stories of these women have been marginalized for a long time and have been reappointed as narratives that emphasize opposition to injustice due to oppressive domination. In evangelism as storytelling, the gospel is embodied in women who do not just repeat the sayings in the holy book but experience

---

29. Stone, *Evangelism after Christendom*, 163.
30. WCC, *Together towards Life*, §6.

and witness the gospel through their language, experiences, critical awareness, and alignment with others who are marginalized. Second, it breaks down the binary view between West and East and seeking strength to work together as a Trinitarian community, namely a postcolonial mission community model that emphasizes just and equal relations. Third, it promotes the concept of martyrdom as a Christian value and virtue, namely presence through friendship and love. Martyrdom as a Christian presence is found in the stories or narratives of the lives of martyrs, especially female martyrs. By understanding martyrdom as a witnessed story, biography is theology.

HANNA BLINDOW: THE TESTIMONY OF A WOMAN MARTYR IN NIAS

Hanna Blindow was born on February 10, 1898, in Germany. Her service in Nias began on October 17, 1930. The initial period, Blindow served in Nias from 1930 to 1936. Then, she was called back by her church to serve in Germany during 1936–1938. She returned to Nias in 1938–1940. From 1940 to 1947, she was exiled in Tokyo, Japan. In 1952, she returned to serve in Nias and died on October 9, 1959. Blindow was buried in the BNKP Hanna Blindow Kindergarten area, in Gunungsitoli City, Indonesia.

Based on her letters to RMG from 1931 onward, Blindow always began her stories with thanksgiving to God. There is a feeling of gratitude because her work is accompanied by God and produces fruit in Nias.

Blindow was the first female missionary to start a girl's school in Nias. The opening of the girls' school took place on June 5, 1931. The opening of this school was attended by parties from mission institutions, the Dutch East Indies government, and the people of Nias. The majority of female students came from Gunungsitoli and the rest came from various areas in northern Nias, southern Nias, and central Nias. They were separated from their parents and hometown. Blindow hoped that by going to school, girls in Nias would get a better and more useful life. For Blindow, this school was a "gift" from God. With gratitude and trust, Blindow believed that this service assignment comes from God alone. Therefore, she worked and prayed, "O God, be our friend, let our hands do this work."[31]

---

31. Blindow, "Letter to Rheinische Missionsgesellschaft" (June 5, 1931), 2.

Prayer, Comforter, and Nurse of the Sick

Blindow was known as a prayer, comforter, and nurse for the sick. In 1932, there was a measles epidemic in Nias that also infected children at a girls' school. A girl named Fatina had a fever of up to forty degrees Celsius. She shouted, "I can't take it anymore. I can't take it anymore." Blindow, who was called *gawe* (an honored woman), prayed to comfort those who were sick. She consoled Fatina by saying, "It's just a day, it's just a night. This disease will pass."

The first girls who were affected by measles were Sarudia and Fatima. Fatima cried and said, "*He inagu, he inagu!*" (O my mother, O my mother). She asked Blindow to take her to her hometown. Fatima was afraid that she would die of measles, while her parents were not with her. The most cheerful girl among them, named Lutiami, also had measles and a high fever. Blindow said to her, "Give me your fever, O Lutiami." She answered, "It will hurt you, *gawe*." She felt pain all over her body, in her head, neck, and stomach. Her tongue and eyes hurt so much. Blindow and other workers tried to nurse and get the sick to have an appetite by bringing them food such as oranges, mangoes, and coconut.

The next day, Blindow saw that Fatima was healthier. The other girls, namely Rosi, Di'ami, Marisa, and Latisa also recovered. Blindow prayed and thanked God. In her letter to RMG, she wrote, "Not only in joy but also in worry, we give thanks that the dangerous disease of measles has passed because we are all with God. We have been given responsibility for these children and God entrusted these sick children to us and for this, we are very grateful for God's help until we were all safe."[32]

Longing for Christmas Traditions in Germany

In her letter to RMG on December 30, 1932, Blindow expressed her longing for her homeland, especially at Christmas. In Nias, it was very difficult for her to imagine the atmosphere of Christmas. In tropical areas like Nias, the sun is always hot, the trees are always green, and the sky is always blue. It was difficult for Germans like Blindow to get the Christmas atmosphere like in her home country.

However, Blindow admitted that the children in Nias had helped her feel Christmas by singing Christmas songs. In the last week of Christmas,

---

32. Blindow, "Letter to Rheinische Missionsgesellschaft" (May 20, 1932), 1.

she promised to tell the girls a Christmas story. Blindow invited them to celebrate Christmas by singing, reading the Bible, and praying. There were also small Christmas gifts for them, such as colored pencils, rubber erasers, and Christmas cards. They were very happy.

On December 2, 1932, they celebrated Christmas. They lit candles and sang several songs such as "Daughter of Zion, Sing." Blindow also told a Christmas story. Ephorus Rabeneck provided opening remarks. From a small island surrounded by the ocean, sweet Christmas songs could be heard.

Crisis and Unbroken Spirit

The early period of developing girls' schools in Nias was a difficult and unprofitable time. The world economy was in crisis, which was called "depression-malaise." The community felt the direct effects of this crisis because it paralyzed and hampered preparations for school construction. When Blindow and her colleagues asked parents to send their daughters to school, they responded, "We have no money. It is a very difficult time." Parents allowed their daughters to go to school if there was a possibility of earning money.[33]

Blindow remained passionate about promoting girls' schools. She conveyed this to the mission station, so that information about the school in Nias was advertised to congregations in Germany so that people would be moved to help. So, school study materials and skills materials were all available free of charge. On July 1, 1931, two classrooms were available, and ten Niasan girls registered. With intensive work supported by a missionary named Borutta, until December 1931, there were around twenty-three girls who registered. Finally, the number of students reached fifty-five.[34]

Girls who were sent by their parents to school were generally still young. There was a reason for this. It was still very early for these young girls to work in the fields to produce rice and potatoes. Parents in Nias found it difficult to send their older daughters because they had to work to help their parents. Another difficulty was that the road to school was not easy to pass. The girls usually went to school together, at least two people. Therefore, if one of the two girls was sick, the other would not go to school

---

33. Blindow, "Letter to Rheinische Missionsgesellschaft" (Dec. 30, 1932), 1.

34. Blindow, "Letter to Rheinische Missionsgesellschaft" (Dec. 30, 1932), 1.

until the sick friend recovered. For this reason, Blindow and her co-workers also often visited girls who did not live in the dormitory.[35]

For Blindow, the Niasan girls who lived in the village were like wood that grows in the forest: they were obedient and loyal to their duties. Blindow believed that this was due only to the power of God working in the human heart. She was very grateful that the help from God and the love of Jesus Christ never fail. What a relief it was for Blindow to see these girls who had previously been stubborn and defiant finally allowing themselves to be led to a good path. In trouble, God does not leave people alone. These girls were very happy to be able to play, sing, and laugh. Blindow felt happy and peaceful with these girls.[36]

Blindow's heart was also very moved when she saw the Niasan girls walking under the heat of the sun to come to school, which was five kilometers from their home. When it heavily rained, they got soaked but still went to school. They were happy because at school they could sing and also make handicrafts.[37]

In addition to schoolwork, Blindow and her colleagues also started work with older village girls in Nias. There were twenty-five girls registered for crafting courses every Thursday afternoon. They enjoyed taking part in this activity and wished the time could be longer. There was a short service that took place when this activity was completed. Blindow was very grateful to God that, only through God's mercy, schools for young girls and vocational work for older girls could be started.[38]

Amid all the difficulties in her ministry, Blindow testified, "We must learn to serve in Nias, to be simple, and so that we do not become tired in this ministry, as long as God entrusts this work to us. How quickly God remembers human work on earth; we are surprised at the wisdom that God gives at the beginning of this work. We remember what happened to our first student in Nias, Rosi, who had been employed by Sister Emilie, but contracted malaria and is now at home in heaven. We have delivered these girls into eternity, while on earth is our great responsibility for the souls of these girls. God accompanies this ministry every day, in the blessing of God's generosity; that is our prayer for the girls in Nias."[39] Amid all these

---

35. Blindow, "Letter to Rheinische Missionsgesellschaft" (Dec. 30, 1932), 1.
36. Blindow, "Letter to Rheinische Missionsgesellschaft" (Dec. 31, 1932), 1.
37. Blindow, "Letter to Rheinische Missionsgesellschaft" (Dec. 31, 1932), 2.
38. Blindow, "Letter to Rheinische Missionsgesellschaft" (Dec. 31, 1932), 2.
39. Blindow, "Letter to Rheinische Missionsgesellschaft" (Dec. 30, 1932), 1.

challenges, what made Blindow's heart glad was that two of her former students were now working at the hospital, and ten of them were nurses at the hospital.

The Future of Girls' Schools

In 1936, after waiting for a long time in uncertainty about moving the girls' school to Gunungsitoli, a decision was finally made. The fact that the work of the Nias girls could continue moved Blindow's heart to gratitude. God had intervened, even though there was no answer yet to the prayers offered. That is why Blindow could only gratefully acknowledge: what an honor it is to serve in this ministry. The condition of the school was not yet good, but God's help was visible. Blindow's embarrassment turned into an opportunity.[40]

Blindow was also grateful to be able to work with local teachers. However, she was concerned about the limitations of their educational formation. They were quite good at teaching, but they did not yet feel the importance of character-building. The teacher's character influences children. For Blindow, one of the main tasks of education is the education of teachers. They should be educated more and in such a way that their personality is formed.[41]

Blindow still believed that if they continued to work regularly, the number of content people would increase. This was Blindow's reason for being joyful in ministry. In the many conversations she had with happy people, Blindow was increasingly moved that they were servants in a far greater sense than could be imagined at all.[42]

Returning Home after Exile

In 1936–1938, Blindow returned to Germany to serve in her church. In 1940–1947, with other missionaries, she was exiled in Tokyo, Japan. She returned to Germany and served in 1947–1952. Blindow was grateful that in 1952, she was sent back to Nias. She was always happy when she saw Nias, which she considered her home. In the early days of returning to Nias,

---

40. Röhm, "Letter to Rheinische Missionsgesellschaft," 1.
41. Röhm, "Letter to Rheinische Missionsgesellschaft," 2.
42. Röhm, "Letter to Rheinische Missionsgesellschaft," 3.

A RECONSTRUCTION OF EVANGELISM FROM A POSTCOLONIAL FEMINIST PERSPECTIVE

Blindow still couldn't believe she was back on this island and asked herself, "Have I not been here for twelve years?"[43]

Many Niasan people came to Blindow and greeted her blissfully. She also felt the joy of meeting people she knew before. She met a former student who was now happy as a young mother. Her other former students also brought their children so Blindow could meet their families. A young mother, thirty years old, brought up her nine children, and among those children were two impressive twins. So, Blindow could imagine how many "grandchildren" she had in Nias.[44]

Some sad stories also happened. Blindow met a young woman who rushed towards her and stroked Blindow's hand while crying. Her name was Sitilia. She was a widow, a young woman whose husband had been killed in a street fight in Sumatra. Sitilia met Blindow with her two small children. Sitilia lived with her mother-in-law.[45]

In the port city area of Gunungsitoli, many young Niasan women carried out their professions as teachers, midwives, nurses, or clerks. Blindow was pleased that her previous work at the girls' school until 1940 had not been in vain. It was like seeing a yellow rice field. The girls who had worked were almost all of Blindow's former students when she was in Nias. They were considered progressive women by the Indonesian Christian Women's Association. Among them, there was an elementary school principal, namely Nuriba Lase. Blindow had known Nuriba for a long time. She was also the one who had helped the Nias church by making an application to RMG to have Blindow recalled to Nias. Blindow and Lase had good communication with each other. There was a big responsibility for Lase; apart from managing the elementary school, Nias girls believed in her as a supporter in times of struggle.[46]

Blindow also paid attention to the struggles of the Niasan youth in overcoming the bride-price problem. The ancient custom of bride-price is still practiced in Nias. The woman's parents, brothers, uncles, and cousins want to earn money from the bride-price. The bride-price is so high that the groom or husband gets into debt later on. Sometimes the grandchildren still have to pay their grandfather's wedding debts. Young people are now trying to overcome this ruinous tradition. Several young girls went to

---

43. Blindow, "Letter to Rheinische Missionsgesellschaft" (Nov. 27, 1952), 1.
44. Blindow, "Letter to Rheinische Missionsgesellschaft" (Nov. 27, 1952), 1.
45. Blindow, "Letter to Rheinische Missionsgesellschaft" (Nov. 27, 1952), 1.
46. Blindow, "Letter to Rheinische Missionsgesellschaft" (Nov. 27, 1952), 1.

Lase. They visited her to ask for protection and help against their greedy parents and brothers. Nuriba helped with many negotiations with supervisory authorities and the government in Gunungsitoli. How happy Nuriba was when she found support and could help them in the right way. These matters were also discussed at Indonesian Christian Women's Association meetings, and Blindow acted as an advisor.[47]

Commencement of the Christian Women's Course

At the second coming of Blindow to Nias, she established the Christian Women's Course (CWC) (Indonesian: *Kursus Wanita Kristen*). Among her letters to RMG in 1953, there was a simple curriculum for the CWC. The following is a list of lessons provided in the course:[48]

Day	Time	Program
Monday	08.00–08.45	Exegesis of Matt 5
	08.45–09.30	Lessons on the New Testament
	09.30–12.00	Housework: washing
	15.00–15.45	Composing/writing work/essays
	15.45–16.30	Lessons on music and gardening
	19.30–20.30	Embroidery course
Tuesday	08.00–08.30	Reading
	08.30–09.30	Diakonia school
	09.30–12.00	Housework: ironing and cooking Indonesian dishes
	15.00–16.30	Lessons on Indonesian and gardening
	19.30–20.30	Singing
Wednesday	08.00–08.45	The story of the Israelites
	08.45–09.30	Lessons on the Old Testament
	09.30–12.00	European cooking and sewing courses
	15.00–15.45	Health lesson
	15.45–16.30	Lessons on music and gardening
	19.30–20.30	Learning to crochet and knit

---

47. Blindow, "Letter to Rheinische Missionsgesellschaft" (Nov. 27, 1952), 2.
48. Blindow, "Letter to Rheinische Missionsgesellschaft" (Jan. 28, 1953), 3.

Day	Time	Program
Thursday	08.00–08.45	Exegesis of Matt 5
	08.45–09.30	Lessons on reading
	09.30–12.00	Indonesian cooking and sewing courses
	15.00–16.30	Lessons on Indonesian and gardening
	19.30–20.30	Embroidery course
Friday	08.00–08.45	Studying the letters of the Bible
	08.45–10.30	Housework: cleaning the house
	11.00–12.30	Bible school at church and prayer time
	15.00–16.30	Women's Bible study group at the hospital
	19.30–20.30	Learning to sing
Saturday	08.00–09.30	Catechism (Sunday school)
	09.30–12.00	Cooking pastries

Succession of Local Women Evangelists: Foundation Testimony

Blindow had an interesting approach to her successor formation. The Nias women whom she taught at CWC were invited to write a letter to RMG that contained a testimony of their service together in evangelism. Fondrusi told the story of a women's course in Tuhemberua, specifically in an area called Lato'i.

Fondrusi wrote that on October 16, 1953, the four of them—Blindow, Somasi, Zami'a, and herself—left Gunungsitoli for Lato'i. In the afternoon, while on the way, about two kilometers past Awa'ai, heavy rain fell and the water was waist high. The car they drove was like a boat on the water. Then, their driver suddenly said, "The car won't move." Fondrusi was worried, and in her heart, she prayed, "Lord, please help our car to run again. We surrender our lives to your hands. Help us to reach to Lato'i." Blindow sat and asked her, "Are you afraid, Fondrusi?" She answered, "God is with us. I am not afraid." Blindow replied, "That's true, my girl." Fondrusi continued, "Then how is this? Should this car be towed?" Blindow replied, "That's impossible." The road behind and around them was full of floodwater. Everyone suddenly fell silent. No one spoke, because everyone prayed in their hearts. Then Fondrusi remembered God's word, "And behold, I am with you always until the end of time." Suddenly the car started again. They then drove towards Tuhemberua, then towards Lato'i. Finally, they arrived at the church and met the pastor of the Fofola congregation in Lato'i.[49]

They were there for six days. Blindow shared the work of evangelism with the three of them. She introduced the Bible text with the theme "Jesus and Disciples." To discuss this theme, some biblical texts were reviewed. They were Matt 4:18–22 (the calling of the disciples); Luke 5:1–11 (Peter the fisherman); John 2:1–11 (wedding at Cana); Mark 4:35–41 (Jesus calms the storm); Mark 8:1–9 (Jesus feeds four thousand people); Acts 9:1–19 (Saul's conversion).[50]

In the afternoon, the four of them gathered with the Niasan women in Lato'i to study the Bible and also pray. Deaconess Somasi led this activity. In the evening there was a short service led by Deaconess Simina.[51]

The pastor in the congregation said that there had been the Great Awakening (revivals) everywhere in Nias, but it had not happened in Lato'i. The women in Lato'i had not experienced an "awakening." It is not easy to bring God's word to the people in Lato'i.[52]

Apart from that, they also visited the sick in Lato'i. There was an interesting experience when they visited Ama Dalifao's family. Ama Dalifao had two wives. His first wife, Ina Fondrusi, was sick at that time. They prayed and read God's word together, "I am the way, the truth, and the life" (John 14:6). Ina Fondrusi cried, and in the end, she admitted that she believed in God. Then the family members wept and said, "How miserable we are if you don't come and show us the way of life!" Then Ama Dalifao handed a magic book into Fondrusi's hands. Then they threw the book into the sea, and Fondrusi said, "I'm not afraid of this book. God guides my feet, and I am not afraid because Jesus is with us."[53] Thus God accompanied the mission journey in Lato'i and gave blessings to that place.

The Seeds of Evangelism by Deaconesses

The deaconess school was started by the BNKP in 1948. There were two reasons to establish the school. First, the example of the Bible Vrouw in the Batak land, Indonesia, inspired the church in Nias. Second, the revival

49. F. Zebua, "Letter to Rheinische Missionsgesellschaft," 1.
50. F. Zebua, "Letter to Rheinische Missionsgesellschaft," 1.
51. F. Zebua, "Letter to Rheinische Missionsgesellschaft," 1.
52. F. Zebua, "Letter to Rheinische Missionsgesellschaft," 2.
53. F. Zebua, "Letter to Rheinische Missionsgesellschaft," 2.

movement that emerged in the Gunungsitoli community at that time caused enthusiasm among women and girls. Pastors in Nias hoped to get help from the women's ministry. In 1948, deaconess training, which lasted only three months, was discontinued. It was seen as less than successful.[54]

BNKP hoped to get a new approach with Blindow's presence in 1952. The church leaders in BNKP promised that the students would later be called back to complete their training so they could provide services to women and children in their village and church. Some were solemnly inducted into the community. For Blindow, this task could not be carried out for long by most deaconesses. According to their statement, some had to struggle with rejection in the church. They waited in vain for the completion of the promised training. Through a visit from Dr. Müller-Krüger in early 1950, the idea arose in them to ask for help from the RMG in Barmen. They were thinking about continuing the delayed deaconess school. This condition supported the idea of asking Blindow to return to Nias. The deaconesses continued to express their concerns to the head of the Nias government and to the BNKP in August 1950. They were assisted by the intercession of Nuriba Lase, who was a former student of Blindow's.[55]

In 1952, Blindow formed a group of sixteen girls from the Gunungsitoli congregation to become deaconesses. While conducting the training, Blindow studied all these issues in the first few weeks after arriving in Nias. She continued to discuss the deaconess school. The BNKP leadership did not think much about this issue and let her alone worry about it. It may have become clear to church leadership that trained deaconesses have the right to work within the congregation and to earn a living. With BNKP's finances in disarray, congregations were unable to support deaconesses. This became clearer as it was revealed at a meeting of praeses (leaders of pastors in a particular area) and pastors of BNKP in Ombölata in March 1955. The proposed deaconess ministry was not approved, although financial means for this were provided by RMG, Germany. At that time, sixteen deaconess candidates were waiting to be placed.[56]

When the BNKP Synod met in May, Blindow wanted to get the agreement of the participants for the final course for deaconesses. The deaconesses had expressed the same request in a letter to the BNKP through Praeses Sohahau Mendröfa. The Nias church did not incur any fees from

---

54. Blindow, "Letter to Rheinische Missionsgesellschaft" (Nov. 20, 1952), 1.
55. Blindow, "Letter to Rheinische Missionsgesellschaft" (Dec. 1, 1953), 2.
56. Blindow, "Letter to Rheinische Missionsgesellschaft" (Dec. 1, 1953), 1.

the course because the funding was approved by RMG management. Then the synod gave its approval to the deaconess graduation course, which took place from June 8 to July 4, 1953, in Ombölata. Blindow was very grateful to Mr. and Mrs. Dr. Thomsen, who willingly supported the ideas carried out by the deaconesses. From August to October 1953, the first two girls did practical deaconess work at the government hospital in Gunungsitoli. In 1955, two more deaconesses could be completed in the next few months.[57]

Now the question arose, how could these deaconesses be employed by the church in ministry? So far nothing had been done by the BNKP church leadership or by the leaders of their respective congregations. Blindow took it as a sign that, in recent months, she had also received numerous requests from churches for Bible courses for women and girls. Through their participation in these courses, deaconesses were introduced to the practice of evangelism. CWC took place in September, October, and December 1955: September 18–22 in Awa'ai, October 16–22 in Tuhemberua, and December 6–13 in Lalai.[58]

Blindow was able to bring a total of ten deaconesses with her to CWC. They discussed topics for women's and girls' classes. These deaconesses acted as "bearers of the good news." Blindow knew from the testimonies she heard about how moved these deaconesses were to minister the word. For Blindow, this may have opened up a path to work for women themselves, which at the time was hampered by a lack of understanding from those responsible for church leadership. Job opportunities for deaconesses had so far been limited to their villages. According to their confessions to Blindow, they were often exploited by several people. Deaconess Fondrusi Zebua had been a weekly prayer woman at BNKP Hilinaa congregation for ten years, and she also served in the children's ministry in BNKP Gunungsitoli. Fondrusi was considered only a "helper," while her spiritual influence also extended beyond her village as she made pastoral visits to the oppressed, poor, and sick. Some deaconesses may still perform such humble service in congregations. They are allowed to participate only in children's services in Gunungsitoli. Despite the difficulties and obstacles in her ministry, when Blindow looked back on the past, she could gratefully admit: "God's goodness is amazing. Those who look to God will be refreshed and their faces will not be ashamed." So God turns shame into an opportunity to serve, and in faith, we hear the beautiful promise, "I myself will go before you and

---

57. Blindow, "Letter to Rheinische Missionsgesellschaft" (Dec. 1, 1953), 2.
58. Blindow, "Letter to Rheinische Missionsgesellschaft" (Dec. 1, 1953), 2.

level mountains, break bronze doors, and break iron bars.... I am the God who created all this" (Isa 45:2, 8).[59]

Encounter with Local Belief

In Blindow's letter in 1954, her views on the culture and local beliefs of the Niasan people were contained. She wrote that in the past, the "pagan" peoples in Nias knew only about the idols whom they worshiped in the rice fields during planting and harvest times. Now, the good news of God's love in Jesus Christ had transformed the lives of living people and filled them with new contentment. The Christian community in Nias praised and glorified God's love and celebrated the anniversary of the birth, death, resurrection, and ascension of Jesus Christ in community services and celebrations. Crowds of Christians, young and old, filled the churches. Blindow quoted the lyrics of a song: "Come, Savior of the unbelievers, redeem, come, most beautiful Sun in this world, let us wait for your light to shine; for God will be born."[60]

However, today the thought of other cultures and religions as "pagan" is considered as a colonial legacy. This section is a criticism of missionary service in the past, both male missionaries and female missionaries, such as Blindow.

Joint Partnership Services with Nias Women

In her ministry, Blindow saw the deaconesses from Nias as partners in joint ministry. The services carried out included the introduction of the Bible, praying, and visiting the sick and elderly. They had many private, one-on-one conversations with women and girls. Blindow was happy in this ministry because God allowed them to witness through their mouths and blessed their ministry.

Blindow heard from many women and girls in Nias who expressed their gratitude for the arrival of deaconesses in their congregations. When Blindow asked them if they wanted deaconesses serving in the congregation, they overwhelmingly agreed. Unfortunately, not one of these fourteen deaconesses was called and employed in BNKP church ministry. What was

---

59. Blindow, "Letter to Rheinische Missionsgesellschaft" (Dec. 1, 1953), 2.
60. Blindow, "Letter to Rheinische Missionsgesellschaft" (Nov. 1, 1954), 1.

the reason? When Blindow spoke with church leaders and the Niasan pastors, they responded that they were not against women's ministry, but there were financial concerns. Pastors and employees, as well as evangelists and church elders, had needed large finances for years because church coffers were empty. How would one or two deaconesses be employed in a church if they were also paid?

Only one of the pastors at Sogaeadu, where Blindow and her colleagues held the final women's course, granted conditional acceptance. During the rice harvest in January, they wanted to collect rice offerings from the women in the congregation, which became the source for providing for the needs of the two deaconesses in Sogaeadu. Blindow was grateful that God had given them a start in deaconess work in a church. These deaconesses and Blindow waited for God's guidance. They had experienced that God's hand had opened so many doors for them to serve during this waiting period.[61]

Services at Hospital

Nursing practice under the leadership of Sister Kate Jüng represented a new path for deaconesses. For three months, two of them worked at Gunungsitoli Hospital. At first, they approached this task with some trepidation, but those fears were soon forgotten. These deaconesses said that they had supporters: "Sister Kate," "Tua Doto," and "Gawe Doto" (Mr. and Mrs. Dr. Thomsen) also opened their hearts to them when they did not know something.

Sitisa, the youngest and last member of the deaconesses, was in the hospital for three months. If a serious illness occurred, there was very little room in the hospital. The hospital was always crowded and also required a lot of servants. Sister Kate provided a place for three deaconesses to help care for the sick, in both the dormitory and the living room.

In southern Nias, there was a diaconia student, namely Za'adi Zebua, who was brought by Sister Margaret Kissing when the relocation occurred. There, she worked in housework and caring for the sick.[62]

---

61. Blindow, "Letter to Rheinische Missionsgesellschaft" (Nov. 8, 1954), 1.
62. Blindow, "Letter to Rheinische Missionsgesellschaft" (Nov. 8, 1954), 2.

A Service Calling to Chinese Girls

An entirely different and new task presented itself to Blindow in the request for lessons and handiwork for the girls of Chinese families. In Gunungsitoli, many Chinese families were living. They made a bright impression. They were also eager to learn. This was proven by their new school building, built in 1957. There was a demand for craft lessons. Blindow gladly accepted this. Blindow started a local school for Chinese girls with two deaconesses, Elise and Somasi. Around twenty Chinese girls came to learn handicrafts in Hilihati.[63]

Plans to Establish a Kindergarten in Gunungsitoli

Blindow considered the establishment of a Protestant kindergarten in Gunungsitoli as an urgent task for the Christian community in Nias. She had discussed this with Mr. Nonnen, government minister of children, during an exchange of letters. Blindow's request was to train two Nias girls as kindergarten workers in Germany so that they could later take over the work of the Christian kindergarten in Nias. Mr. Nonnen proposed to train teachers in Indonesia only.[64]

After exploring for some time, Blindow saw an opportunity to send two prospective kindergarten teachers to Padang, West Sumatra. The Indonesian government had started work on the kindergarten school, and the state training center for kindergarten teachers was located in Padang. So far, Padang was the only training location in all of Sumatra. There, participants consisted of all ethnicities and religions in Sumatra. Meanwhile, if prospective teachers trained in Germany, there were special advantages because they had a background in the Christian world. Blindow saw role models in the basic Protestant character. For this reason, Blindow asked the RMG to train two Nias girls as kindergarten teachers. Finally, two prospective teachers were sent to Padang, and two persons were sent to Barmen, Germany. Blindow hoped that a Protestant kindergarten would soon be built in Nias.[65]

---

63. Blindow, "Letter to Rheinische Missionsgesellschaft" (Nov. 8, 1954), 2.
64. Blindow, "Letter to Rheinische Missionsgesellschaft" (Dec. 1, 1955), 1–2.
65. Blindow, "Letter to Rheinische Missionsgesellschaft" (Dec. 1, 1955), 3.

Attention to Youth Ministry

In her letter in 1957, Blindow stated that work among women in the Nias Christian community had shifted over the last two years to youth work with ministry among Nias deaconesses. There was a spiritual awakening of the islanders in Indonesia. The fact that young people were particularly affected was also an unmistakable sign of the independence efforts young people on Nias Island were experiencing in Indonesia. Christian communities must not neglect their duties towards these spiritually awakened youth.[66]

Blindow testified, "You own the time, O God. Also, lift the burdens of this year and turn them into blessings. Now in Jesus Christ, we will firmly and confidently achieve the goal."[67]

Last Letter

Blindow wrote her last letter to RMG before she was stricken with a fatal illness. In that letter, Blindow wrote with a grateful heart the first annual report on the work of the established Home Bible School in Gunungsitoli. Blindow rejoiced to see the new school buildings brightly painted and surrounded by beds of flowers shining like jewels. This building was connected to the church building, indicating that this school belonged to BNKP. For Blindow, this stage was BNKP "development," namely: progress or development work in the Nias church.[68]

DOROTHEA RICHTER: THE TESTIMONY OF A FRIENDSHIP OPENER

Dorothea Richter was born on May 18, 1928, in Nünberg, Germany. She served in Nias from June 14, 1959. She was sent to Nias and placed at CWC and BNKP Hanna Blindow Kindergarten until 1990. In 1991, she retired and returned to Germany. She died on November 29, 1998, in her hometown of Nünberg.

---

66. Blindow, "Letter to Rheinische Missionsgesellschaft" (Dec. 30, 1957), 1.
67. Blindow, "Letter to Rheinische Missionsgesellschaft" (Dec. 30, 1957), 2.
68. Blindow, "Letter to Rheinische Missionsgesellschaft" (Dec. 30, 1958), 1.

Friendship with Hanna Blindow: A Testimony

In 1959, Dorothea Richter had to face a harsh reality. A friend who was supposed to guide her in ministry in Nias, Hanna Blindow, had passed away. For Richter, the experience of losing Blindow was decisive for the continuity of her ministry in Nias. In mid-August 1959, Blindow had been diagnosed with severe carcinoma. Until then, Blindow had still been on full duty even with the last of her strength. In September, Blindow had had surgery, and Richter had had more time to care for her.

Richter was grateful for the opportunity to be at Blindow's bedside during her final hours. Richter could talk to her more about further work. They both looked forward to doing another course together and thought that until then perhaps a replacement for Blindow from Germany would come along. In two years of wonderful collaboration, Blindow had introduced Richter to the Niasan religious services and language with so much understanding and love. For Richter, Blindow had shown her what this meant: "Living is Christ." In the final weeks of Blindow's life, Richter experienced the reality of the second term: "Dying is gain." These sentences were written on Blindow's gravestone on October 9, 1959.[69]

Continuing the Work of CWC

Richter continued the service at CWC which had been started by Blindow. The first course, which had started on January 2, 1958, was able to continue without hindrance, even though the situation in Indonesia was volatile. The second course started in August and ended in February 1958. In the second course, the participants were mostly daughters of teachers, civil servants, and predominantly daughters of church employees (praeses, pastors, and evangelists). The third course started in March and ended in early September 1959. Participants in the third course were mostly daughters of village heads. Despite their parents' occupation, these girls were mostly village children. Half of the participants had completed elementary school. The struggle that Richter experienced was that there were always more participants registered than she could accept. The participant quota prioritized two girls from each of the twelve districts of the Nias church.[70]

---

69. Richter, "Letter to Rheinische Missionsgesellschaft" (Dec. 29, 1958), 1.
70. Richter, "Letter to Rheinische Missionsgesellschaft" (Dec. 29, 1958), 1.

Encounters with Chinese Girls

A Chinese Christian woman asked Richter: "Why not take care of our girls?" Although Richter and her colleagues didn't care much about this at first, they were eventually touched by the question. In early December 1960, they began knitting courses that took place three times a week. Among seventeen Chinese girls, only two were Christians. Richter and her colleagues' goal was to reach those who did not yet believe. At the beginning of each class period, Richter and her colleagues sang with the Chinese children and listened to Bible stories. There was an interesting experience with these Buddhist girls because Richter celebrated Christmas with them. Richter also had the opportunity to take Bible stories in Indonesian to various Chinese homes. They had fun at Christmas celebrations with the deaconesses, women from the Bible study class, and previous CWC alumni. For Richter, working for Chinese princesses was very enjoyable.[71]

Service for the Niasan Girls

For Richter, her ministry in Nias was about making evangelism possible. Her purpose was that young women in Nias could experience the power of the living word of God through education. Richter was not alone in this ministry work. During her service, she received more support from BNKP leadership, namely Ephorus Sohahau Mendröfa. Richter was very grateful for the good relationship with Ephorus, especially after the loss of Blindow. By having a good relationship with church leadership, Richter was able to discuss all questions and assess others' work, specifically regarding the admission and release of students. Ephorus knew these girls because he also taught Bible studies. Ephorus's daughter also helped teach the Indonesian language as one of the subjects. The missionary's wife, Mrs. Kosack, helped with choir and catechism lessons. Richter was very grateful for all this help. Richter also taught some subjects, such as the New and Old Testaments, cooking, sewing, knitting, and embroidery. Sometimes Richter felt all this work was beyond her strength.[72]

In 1959, Richter met participants who could speak in tongues. During the course, a girl had a "magic book" with her, but then she was won by

---

71. Richter, "Letter to Rheinische Missionsgesellschaft" (Jan. 7, 1961), 2.
72. Richter, "Letter to Rheinische Missionsgesellschaft" (Jan. 7, 1961), 1.

A RECONSTRUCTION OF EVANGELISM FROM A POSTCOLONIAL FEMINIST PERSPECTIVE

Jesus. It was not an easy struggle for her to free herself from this book. The magic book contained several things that had been revealed to herself.[73]

While serving at CWC, Richter also saw the importance for Nias girls to get to know other communities who rejoice under God's word. Some new and stronger relationships with society resulted from the experience of meeting other girls from Japan and China who came to Nias. Richter also enjoyed attending meetings of small Chinese congregations. Batak women's associations often asked her to serve them. Richter continued to make individual visits because she felt more connected to the service of one-on-one visits with other women.[74]

Richter looked at her first years in Nias with gratitude for all God's grace in her service. She was grateful for the many open doors and opportunities. Due to the large number of services, Richter was often stressed because she did not have the time and energy to do enough to take advantage of all these opportunities.[75]

At CWC, Richter saw the potential of the Niasan women. It was very exciting for her. The perseverance of the Niasan girls could be seen in their written works. They showed extraordinary enthusiasm. Apart from writing, they cooked with limited ingredients. She hoped that this knowledge would also be in line with the Bible lessons that entered the hearts of these students, that the word of God would be planted "into their heart like a plant" with strong roots, growing and bearing fruit.[76]

In November 1960, Catholic nuns began working in Nias. Eight of them were placed in Gunungsitoli. Their main service was visiting Chinese families to advertise the Catholic kindergarten, which opened on April 2, 1960. In January 1960, there were more than one hundred children enrolled. Meanwhile, after a satisfactory start, Richter was somewhat disappointed with the further development of the kindergarten work at BNKP. The main struggle was that the number of children had increased only to forty. Half of the children had moved to Catholic kindergartens. The exact number could not be determined because the location was small and had a limited class. Another struggle was that kindergarten teachers at BNKP did not put their whole hearts into this ministry and wanted to quit after their service contracts expired. Some were getting married, others wanted

---

73. Richter, "Letter to Rheinische Missionsgesellschaft" (Dec. 27, 1959), 2.
74. Richter, "Letter to Rheinische Missionsgesellschaft" (Dec. 1, 1963), 2.
75. Richter, "Letter to Rheinische Missionsgesellschaft" (Dec. 1, 1963), 1.
76. Richter, "Letter to Rheinische Missionsgesellschaft" (Jan. 9, 1963), 1.

to study in Jakarta. During this period of struggle, Richter did not know how she could survive with two jobs, one service at CWC and one service at BNKP kindergarten.[77]

Richter and other ministers had not yet seen clearly how the Catholic nuns' counter-labor would look in detail. They had heard that there would be four people in charge of kindergarten work, and others would be involved in courses and boarding school work at the Catholic church. The result would probably be similar to the service at BNKP. Richter hoped that they did not let themselves be drawn into competitive ministry but continued working joyfully and trusting in God's promises. In the following years, the work of CWC and kindergarten was smoother. Richter had even thought about how to reach the Niasan community in southern Nias. The main obstacle in southern Nias was that young girls were generally married.[78]

Some Challenges

For the CWC, Richter saw that the challenge was that the girls sent by their parents were too young. This made Bible study difficult. In practical subjects, they could follow the Bible study. Ephorus came once a week for such study. Ephorus's daughter taught Indonesian language lessons. Amina Zega provided health education. Somasi, who was in charge of the dorm, taught drawing lessons by heart. Richter was grateful for the individual hard work, especially for the pleasant collaboration with Somasi, who worked with Richter for six years.[79]

The need for educated young people was increasing. This was demonstrated by some sad incidents among school teenagers in the past year. These young people were like someone who was trying to break away from old habits and still had no new ground. Would that the young people could find true freedom in their bond with Jesus Christ! Richter was very grateful for the open and happy community with female students and also the good relationships with their parents. In addition, there were about eighty Japanese, Chinese, and Malaysian girls, more than half of them non-Christian,

---

77. Richter, "Letter to Rheinische Missionsgesellschaft" (Jan. 7, 1961), 2.
78. Richter, "Letter to Rheinische Missionsgesellschaft" (Jan. 7, 1961), 2.
79. Richter, "Letter to Rheinische Missionsgesellschaft" (Dec. 30, 1963), 1.

who came twice a week. They joined CWC for craft lessons, to hear Bible stories, and to learn Christian hymns.[80]

When the ninth CWC course was held, Richter formed an alumni group. The members were those who had returned to the village. Their numbers were increasing. She thanked God for giving strength and grace to the ministry so far. Richter also believed that their service was getting better among the Niasan girls. At CWC, they could learn to understand each other better. The participants were also able to recognize cultural and national differences but were still united by togetherness in God's church.[81]

Richter was also increasingly open to little girls who wanted to learn. In the ninth CWC course, there were twenty-seven little girls, including four from southern Nias and two from Batu Island. The difference between the Nias language and the Batu Islands language brought several happy moments to their community. There were some young women aged eighteen to twenty-two years. Their presence also appealed to younger people. In general, this course was a great group and especially open minded. Richter had rarely experienced Bible study with such joy.[82]

Gratitude

Richter was grateful for everything that had happened in the past. She thanked God for several miracles that had enabled them to continue serving in Nias. Above all, God had given time for churches in Indonesia to develop. Richter celebrated God's great deeds in protecting the community on the island of Nias. She prayed that she could still use the time she had to serve more. Richter's desire was for young people to find an anchor in Jesus Christ and be able to endure life's struggles. Richter was deeply moved by what would happen to the churches in Nias, especially to the youth.[83]

Richter was happy when, at one gathering with girls, she heard a conversation between these young people. One said, "Jesus Christ, he is not there, he has risen!" There was also one girl who testified loudly, "And I will remain a Christian! I just prayed under my mosquito net, where no one saw me." These statements of faith brought Richter joy.[84]

80. Richter, "Letter to Rheinische Missionsgesellschaft" (Dec. 30, 1963), 1.
81. Richter, "Letter to Rheinische Missionsgesellschaft" (Jan. 18, 1965), 2.
82. Richter, "Letter to Rheinische Missionsgesellschaft" (Jan. 18, 1965), 1.
83. Richter, "Letter to Rheinische Missionsgesellschaft" (Jan. 18, 1965), 3.
84. Richter, "Letter to Rheinische Missionsgesellschaft" (Jan. 13, 1966), 1.

Concerns for Fellow Niasan Women

Richter held camps for CWC alumni. She used this opportunity to share stories about life and ministry among women. Richter heard about several alumni who had difficult lives. Richter felt how much they needed strength. One of the alumni said, "I rarely get the opportunity to read God's word quietly. Our little home was divided into two rooms. Our family lives with a grandmother who has mental problems. She cursed and screamed most of the day. Every morning at four a.m., I go looking for food for the pigs. When should I find solitude to read God's word?" Other alumni also talked about their lives. One had become the wife of a sixteen-year-old man. Her husband couldn't stand the marriage and immediately ran away. Another told about the long journey she had traveled on foot. In the alumni meeting, Richter invited them to discuss the story of Elijah in the Bible and hoped that the women who had become alumni could become people who stood before God like Elijah in times of trouble.[85]

Hospitality: An Opportunity to Share God's Word

CWC received guests such as priests, students from technical schools in Sumatra, students from secondary schools from Telukdalam, or women who came to wait for educational connections and temporarily wanted to study courses in making mosquito nets, sheets, blankets, or curtains. They were also visited by guests from the ecumenical group, namely the team from the Communion of Churches in Indonesia (CCI). Richter was happy to get to know Indonesian Christians from other islands with an ecumenical vision. They were visited by the Ephorus of the church in China many times. CWC received groups of young sports teachers from Bali or young priests from Halmahera. There were also workers from the Salvation Army who came to visit.[86]

For Richter, hosting these guests was an opportunity to connect with other churches. Getting to know the community outside BNKP was important for the Nias church so that they could grow their responsibility for other people who had not received the message of God's word.[87]

---

85. Richter, "Letter to Rheinische Missionsgesellschaft" (Jan. 13, 1966), 2.
86. Richter, "Letter to Rheinische Missionsgesellschaft" (Jan. 13, 1966), 3.
87. Richter, "Letter to Rheinische Missionsgesellschaft" (Jan. 13, 1966), 3.

SONIA PARERA-HUMMEL: THE MISSIONARY'S WIFE IS A MISSIONARY

Sonia Parera-Hummel is the wife of a missionary, namely Uwe Hummel.[88] When Hummel was sent by UEM to be a missionary in Nias, Parera participated. Parera is an Indonesian woman who comes from Moluccas. So, it was easier for her to adapt to the Indonesian context, although there were challenges because Nias has a very different culture from her home culture. Parera was happy to come to Nias because, for her, she enjoyed seeing other parts of Indonesia. Before going to Nias, Parera read several books about Nias. In preparation for going to Nias, she also had discussions with missionary wives who had been to Nias, such as Annemarie Topperwien, Ruth Kozack, and Helbog Schekatz.

Parera served in Nias from February 1995 to June 2001. Initially, she served in Gunungsitoli at the Teacher Preacher School. Parera's services increased in Nias; for example, she was asked to give lectures and sermons in several congregations in Gunungsitoli. Another service she carried out was being chairman of the BNKP scholarship team. Parera also became the first librarian of the Teacher Preacher School, which was the forerunner of BNKP Sundermann Theological Seminary in Nias. Together with Uwe, Parera taught as a lecturer at the seminary in Nias. They were trying to ensure that students received "mini-library" packages from BNKP partners in Gladbach-Neuss, Germany.

To provide service to fellow women pastors, Parera formed a group called Eunike. The members of the group were not only from BNKP but also from other denominations such as AMIN and ONKP. Parera also formed the Peniel Singers, a vocal group for the youth. This group consisted of more than forty members in Gunungsitoli. They were trained to speak English by singing English songs.

Before coming to Nias, Parera worked as a lecturer. She taught Greek, New Testament, and systematic theology at the Halmahera Church Theological School in Ternate, North Moluccas. Parera still loves teaching. She believes that in any society, education is the key to transforming and improving the quality of life.

Parera observed that the Niasan love to discuss things, but the Niasan women were still "ashamed to express their opinions." In fact, according to Parera's observations, many Niasan women are intelligent and critical.

---

88. This section draws on my interview with Sonia Parera-Hummel, Sept. 30, 2020.

Apart from that, some are plain and "shy," perhaps because they were forged by a hard life and by customs that are not always in favor of women.

In Nias, Parera also noticed that children with "special needs" were considered a disgrace in the family. They are hidden in the house and are never socialized. This condition is very different than the experience of Parera, who also has an autistic son. In Germany and the Netherlands, autistic children are gaining acceptance. This worrying condition prompted Parera to establish a "special class" for children with disabilities at the BNKP Hanna Blindow Kindergarten. Disabled children are also given special time to join other classes so that other children can learn to interact with them socially. Parera also visited parents' homes to persuade them to send their disabled children to the BNKP Hanna Blindow Kindergarten. Unfortunately, not everyone wants to. There was a person in a government position in Nias who once sent his son, but after a few months, the child was taken away again because he was "embarrassed."

When she was principal at BNKP Hanna Blindow Kindergarten, Parera implemented a cross-subsidy system. Children from parents who can afford to pay more support the less able families. At that time, Parera compiled three to five categories of school fees. In the beginning, other kindergarten teachers rejected this new system, but after it was implemented it turned out that the financial condition was in surplus. The kindergarten cash book is placed in the office so that everyone can see the money coming in and going out transparently. If there is a need for building construction, BNKP Hanna Blindow Kindergarten holds a bazaar on Sundays at the BNKP congregation in Gunungsitoli City.

Parera also taught at STT BNKP Sundermann in Nias. At that time, there was no specific curriculum designed according to student interests. Parera admitted that this was their shortcoming at that time. Each lecturer taught according to their duties. Some lecturers had never taught the subjects and simply copied what they had been taught at other campuses. At that time, there were no regular meetings to discuss the agreed-upon curriculum.

Despite the limitations, BNKP Sundermann Seminary is a blessing for many Niasan women, especially those who want to go to further school but are not allowed to leave Nias Island by their parents. Before 1990, the number of Nias women who were allowed to leave the island for further studies was very small. Apart from the cost factor, this also happens because of the patriarchal confines of the Niasan customs. Parera assessed that students at BNKP Sundermann Seminary were generally diligent. Of course, there are some weak ones. However, according to Parera's observations, this was mostly caused by existing "mental obstacles." They are wired to believe that their abilities are limited. Of course, this is completely untrue. Changing mindsets is hard work. Parera observed that the Niasan women generally have the character of being willing to sacrifice, willing to give in, fatalistic, and guilty if they think they are not in line with the majority.

When Parera arrived in Nias, there were women pastors who, even though they had been ordained, were not yet considered independent by the synod leadership to be responsible for leading the congregation. Even though they had been ordained for years, they only became "assistants" of male pastors. During the time of BNKP Ephorus (synod leader) Bazatulö Christian Hulu, Parera revealed this problem. Hulu had studied in Germany and understood German language and culture. Parera and her husband exchanged many ideas with him. The case of the "functional pastor" really touched Parera's heart. This was a theme that she repeatedly voiced subtly to the BNKP leadership at that time. Parera was happy because lately there was the first female BNKP pastor who was ordained as leader of a congregation, named Rev. Miseria Daeli.

The pastors' meeting in 1996 in Gunungsitoli was quite memorable for Parera. At the end of the meeting, participants elected ten pastors as representatives at the Synod Assembly. Previously, there had never been a woman pastor representing the pastor corps, even though there were already several female pastors in BNKP. Parera observed this. She approached the female pastors and specifically spoke with the pastor Nurulia Ziliwu so that she could gather all the female pastors and vicars to meet and have a heart-to-heart discussion at the Debora dormitory. When asked for her views during the meeting, Parera said, "It is time for you to leave an example for future generations. History must record that some women pastors represented the BNKP pastors corps. Let's just elect one woman first so that at least out of the ten members, there is one woman." Discussions took place, but almost everyone refused to volunteer. Finally, Miseria Daeli suggested that the oldest female pastor come forward, because she was already known and at the same time this was also a sign of respect for her. Everyone finally agreed. Then Parera proposed a "strategy" so that female candidates would win. These women pastors began contacting all the male pastors about their ideas, and potential women pastors were being considered as members of the synod boards. Apart from that, during the forum, Nurulia Ziliwu was also supported by other female pastors to speak at the forum. Finally, for the first time, a female pastor was elected to represent the BNKP pastor corps at the 1997 BNKP Synod Assembly. For Parera, women pastors at BNKP learn and grow quickly from their positive experiences and also have amazing solidarity.

In Eunike meetings, namely discussion forums between female pastors initiated by Parera and usually held at Parera's house in Hilihati every month, female pastors talked a lot about challenges in ministry. Eunike also became a heart-to-heart forum, where they strengthened and motivated each other. Slowly but surely, there were no more voices from under the pulpit shouting, "Hey woman, get down from there, you're dirty" (experience of a female BNKP pastor). Parera's final message to Eunike's group was "Don't disappoint your younger sisters. Make a way for them too."

For Parera, there is historical injustice towards female missionaries. According to her, missionaries in Nias and elsewhere always built schools first. They were formal educators. The missionaries' wives and nuns were the most devoted educators in these schools. Unfortunately, their names are rarely mentioned in the church's history.

MASRIAL ZEBUA: A FIRST WOMAN MISSIONARY FROM NIAS TO THE PHILIPPINES

One of the first local woman missionary figures from Nias was Masrial Zebua. In her writing about her experience of being a missionary among the Manobo people, in the Philippines, Zebua begins by asking about the purpose of her life. She asked, "What do I live for?" Zebua's desire to become a missionary emerged when she learned in the Sunday School story about Jesus being crucified because of human sins. This story meant a lot to Zebua. According to her belief, if sins are forgiven, humans can enter heaven if they ask Jesus Christ. Zebua remembered those who still don't know who Jesus Christ is. How can they be saved? Zebua was called to become a missionary because she had compassion for people who did not know Jesus. She said, "I live to be a missionary, to glorify God. My life is a treasure that I cannot exchange for anything. To work in God's field, that's what I live for!"[89]

In her writing, Zebua describes her encounter with the local Manobo people. At first, it was difficult for Zebua to communicate directly with

---

89. M. Zebua, *Sampah menjadi Persembahan*, 11.

A RECONSTRUCTION OF EVANGELISM FROM A POSTCOLONIAL FEMINIST PERSPECTIVE

them because the language was difficult to learn. Apart from that, understanding the character of the Manobo people was also not easy. The adults were indifferent, and the children were annoying. They were dirty, smelly, and undisciplined. Animal and human waste was scattered everywhere. Animal cages and houses were difficult to distinguish. The Manobo women often fought, the men were drunk, and they like to steal. The head of the local subdistrict also considered the Manobo people lazy. They liked to steal, drink, gamble, and cause trouble.[90]

It was the Manobo community that Zebua served. The first activities she did were praying, showering the children, providing drinking water from a pump, learning languages, and preaching the truth of God's word. Zebua saw a challenge to the gospel message from the spirit-worshiping sect in Tuguangu. Zebua described the sect as the hand of the evil. The Manobo people had been "snared," and Zebua prayed that Jesus Christ would "take them back."[91]

For motivation for her evangelism strategy, Zebua set a target. She prayed that in December 2000, the entire Taguagu village (sixty families, so four hundred people) would receive salvation in the Lord Jesus Christ. Goals for church planting are very visible. They lead to church planting, significant numbers of souls, and a confession of faith in Jesus Christ.[92]

Zebua's ongoing strategy for preaching the gospel was intensive gospel preaching and discipleship. Initially, she chose twelve co-workers, consisting of six men and six women to "capture" other youths and teenagers in the ministry. A Taguagu youth was discipled and sent to study to be a missionary at the Evangelism Explosion (EE) agency and the Inter-Christian University Fellowship (IFES). The initial results of this work were four new members. The members continued to increase until after four months there were fifteen people, and after seven months, there were one hundred members.[93]

Zebua's experiences as a missionary were quite interesting. She once prayed for the healing of a young man named Matet. Later, Matet was called to teach other children to pray. Zebua also met a man named Daniel, who was a drunkard. After hearing the gospel, Daniel changed for the better. There is also the story of a man named Magonot, who was a spirit

---

90. M. Zebua, *Sampah menjadi Persembahan*, 56–60.
91. M. Zebua, *Sampah menjadi Persembahan*, 60.
92. M. Zebua, *Sampah menjadi Persembahan*, 65.
93. M. Zebua, *Sampah menjadi Persembahan*, 66.

worshiper. After receiving the gospel, Magonot became a believer in Jesus. There is a story about Rosita who was sick, but before she died she accepted Jesus. Rosita was sure that she would go to heaven.[94]

At the end of her book, Zebua reflects that the village of Taguagu in the Philippines, which was once "garbage" (all the evils were there: drunkenness, gambling, laziness, gossip, quarreling, stupid, poor, stubbornness, stealing) had been transformed into "offerings" to God. For Zebua, Manobo land is God's reaping field, and fifty thousand souls await deliverance from the devil's hand.[95]

In the gospel message, Zebua focused her theology on the doctrine of salvation. This salvation is told in the creation narrative (Gen 1–2); the fall (Gen 3; 1 John 5:19; Isa 59:2; Eph 2:1, 5; Rom 3:23; 6:23a); salvation (John 3:16–17; Matt 1:18–23; Luke 1:19–32; John 1:1, 14; Rom 6:23); the work of Jesus the Savior (1 Cor 15:3; 2 Cor 5:21; 1 Pet 2:24; John 6:47; 2 Tim 2:8); and living as children of God (Acts 4:12).[96]

The story of Zebua that she wrote was welcomed as good news at BNKP. Zebua narrated her life story in the form of storytelling. Women like Masrial Zebua even dared to write their narratives, and their stories became an inspiration for other Nias women.

DESTALENTA ZEGA: NIAS WOMAN MISSIONARY AT WORLDWIDE EVANGELIZATION FOR CHRIST (WEC)

The second female missionary figure from Nias is Destalenta Zega.[97] She was born in Gunungsitoli on December 31, 1969. She served as a pastor in Nias from 1995 to 1997. Then she was sent to serve in Sending WEC Indonesia (SWI) (1997–1998), WEC England (1999–2000), mission ministry in Kyrgyzstan (2000–2005), chairman of SWI (2005–2014), and treasurer of SWI (2014 to present). SWI is an interdenominational mission agency, a branch of WEC International, which is currently headquartered in Singapore. SWI's ministry target is to reach tribes who have not heard the gospel outside Indonesia. Only SWI members who have fulfilled various requirements and training can be sent to countries outside Indonesia. Currently, WEC International serves around one hundred ethnic groups in ninety

---

94. M. Zebua, *Sampah menjadi Persembahan*, 80.

95. M. Zebua, *Sampah menjadi Persembahan*, 139.

96. M. Zebua, *Sampah menjadi Persembahan*, 151–55.

97. This section draws on my interview with Destalenta Zega, Nov. 28, 2022.

countries. WEC International members currently consist of around two thousand workers who come from various countries and different church backgrounds but have the same vision, namely reaching neglected ethnic groups in the world.

Zega decided to become a missionary in 1993 when there was a mission service on her campus. There was a missionary from Germany presenting about an ex-Soviet Union country. At that time, the missionary challenged the participants by asking who wanted to go. All the students were silent. Zega sat praying, but in her heart, she was restless, as if the challenge was facing her. However, Zega had not taken the step to say, "Yes, it's me," but she just prayed until the service was over and didn't want to look up. She just bowed her head and prayed. As time went by, the call continued to ring in Zega's ears, until finally she was reminded that if German missionaries had not come to Nias, the people of Nias would not have heard the gospel until now. This increasingly challenged Zega that it was time for Nias people to take the gospel to other places.

While at college, Zega studied more and socialized with missionaries who came from various countries. She was truly blessed by the simplicity of their daily lives, humility, patience, and respect for each student. Zega saw what they taught and said reflected in the testimony of their daily lives.

For Zega, evangelism is the process of preaching the gospel or delivering the news of salvation to people who don't know or don't believe in God. The goal is that those who do not yet know God can decide to believe and become disciples of Christ. For example, when serving in Kyrgyzstan, Zega's ministry focus had been to reach people who did not know Christ or had never heard the meaning of the gift of salvation from the Lord Jesus. The methods she used were through friendship, personal conversations, inviting them to her home, or playing and teaching children to sing.

The context in Nias, specifically at BNKP, is different than other regions. In Nias, people know Christ. Meanwhile, WEC serves those who do not know Christianity at all. They have never even read the Bible. Therefore, in different contexts, different methods of evangelism are also suitable. According to Zega, in the BNKP context, proper evangelism is a personal conversation or visit. She added that nowadays, evangelism is more meaningful if it is done through friendship and personal conversations. If you can't meet in person, you can also use social media, for example, to send reflections or verses from God's word.

What needs to be considered in evangelism is that the messenger has experienced and lived out the grace of God that has been received in her life. What testimony can we give to the people we want to serve if we have never experienced and felt God's grace in our lives? Then, courage, vigilance, and wisdom are also needed. The obstacles that Zega has experienced in evangelizing include feelings of fear of rejection, limited time, and duties and responsibilities at the office and also at home as a wife and mother of children.

For Zega, evangelism is not only about giving but also receiving from others. When she was carrying out mission service in Kyrgyzstan, Zega evangelized a neighbor next door while telling about the love of the Lord Jesus who atones for human sins. At the same time, Zega also learned from her about how to milk a cow. Through practical things like this, a warmer communication atmosphere is created.

For Zega, some things can also be learned from former Western missionaries. For example, the missionaries received full support from the church that sent them. Westerners are highly valued and respected by Indonesians, so it is easy for them to evangelize. They are also equipped with various skills, making it easy to enter areas that seem difficult to reach. The downside is that Western culture becomes prominent in the places they serve, for example, the way liturgy and services are brought from their country, such as the shape of the church building. In addition, because the Western world is considered rich, the congregations that have been served hope only for donors from outside but do not think about how to finance their lives from within. If we compare evangelism in BNKP today, according to Zega, there is a part of evangelism that is lame. The evangelism carried out by BNKP currently focuses more on diaconia. Meanwhile, there is still very little direct evangelism to people who do not yet believe in God.

Zega hopes that in the future more women will be involved in evangelism. Nowadays, women's involvement in evangelization is quite growing. It is women who take on many of these responsibilities, especially being missionaries outside Indonesia. Currently, many women have self-confidence and potential. According to Zega, in the past women found it difficult to decide to get involved in evangelism. There is a feeling of fear of rejection and so on. Now, many women are involved in evangelizing, not only for their tribe but also daring to go outside their tribe and even outside their country.

YANI SAOIYAGÖ: INTERNAL MISSIONARY FOR THE NIASAN PEOPLE

Yani Saoiyagö was born on January 7, 1967.[98] She was ordained a pastor at BNKP in 1993. Her first placement was as functional pastor in the Lahewa district, northern Nias. During the vicariate period, Saoiyagö served at the Mission and Ecumenical Commission (KMO) in the BNKP Synod Office. At that time, KMO was formed specifically for evangelism ministry, personal ministry, and mission seminars.

Saoiyagö specifically had a connection with KMO BNKP when she was still a student at Tanjung Enim Seminary. At that time, KMO BNKP had a network with several theological colleges outside Nias. When Saoiyagö completed her undergraduate studies in theology, the KMO asked the synod to place her to serve at the KMO. Together with her mentor, Rev. Manaö, Saoiyagö served at KMO for approximately six months.

Saoiyagö has known KMO since she was a junior high school student. She remembers that at that time, there was a group of young people from Bandung who carried out evangelization at her church in the Idanögawo area. The evangelistic activities carried out by these young people impressed her. Since then, Saoiyagö became interested in evangelism and was also called to serve God. At a very young age, she asked what was the purpose of human life if not to serve God.

At KMO, Saoiyagö and other fellow ministers carried out evangelistic services by traveling around the island of Nias. Evangelism programs carried out include spiritual awakening services, personal services, seminars, family services, and children's services. According to Saoiyagö, evangelism is a service to make someone aware of existence before God and also the end of human life before God. One of the powers of darkness at that time still existed among the people of Nias who had amulets. During personal evangelistic ministry, they repented of their way of living in darkness. This evangelism touched many Nias peoples so that they understood better how to live in Christ. The people they served were already Christians, but they were not yet strong in the faith. Evangelism strengthens them even more. Saoiyagö serves the Batu islands, Susua, Lahusa, and also the Ma'u.

The challenges of evangelism for Saoiyagö were quite pronounced at the beginning of her ministry, especially because she was a woman. In Nias culture, men are more dominant, so there is a gap between female and

---

98. This section draws on my interview with Yani Saoiyagö, Nov. 11, 2022.

male pastors. At one time during her service, a male elder asked her, "Isn't your husband angry because you are always away for ministry and rarely at home?" Saoiyagö was quite surprised to receive such a question because her husband and family support her in her ministry. Saoiyagö asked back, "Why do you ask me something like that?" The male elder said, "If I were your husband, I would not allow my wife to be out of the house too much for service. Moreover, you are also often carried by motorbike taxis in the service." (In the early days of her service, Saoiyagö often used motorbike taxis to reach difficult service areas.) Hearing this statement, Saoiyagö replied, "Thank God you are not my husband. In marriage, partners should know each other's work so that regrets and arguments do not arise. My husband knows my job as a pastor. In this service, we sacrifice all of our time, energy, thoughts, and even material things. Apart from that, communication within the family is important so that our partners do not lose trust in us." That was one of Saoiyagö's experiences as a woman pastor. She is very grateful that her husband and children fully support her ministry.

In facing challenges in the field, Saoiyagö also does not give up, because she relies on prayer, the word of God, mastering church regulations, and strategies for approaching the community. Therefore, visiting church members is important. According to Saoiyagö, women have the power to build relationships and invite congregation members to participate according to their talents in ministry. Women also have the strength to be strong, have a big soul, and not hold grudges. When there are challenges, anyone who wants to hinder them is not seen as an enemy but as a ministry partner who still needs guidance.

For the current BNKP context, Saoiyagö considers that the evangelism model like Evangelism Explosion is good, but the problem is that not all participants who take part in the training are called to continue this evangelism. Saoiyagö saw the potential for Nias women to become evangelists, because women have the power to build networks with other women. Apart from that, one method of evangelism that can be carried out by women is personal visits to fellow women, because that way they can chat and get to know their struggles and how God's word can help them in their struggles. One verse of God's word from the Gospel of Mark 16:15 that accompanied Saoiyagö in her ministry was the verse she received when she was on trial, "Go into all the world, preach the gospel to every creature." Since then, Saoiyagö believed that "seek God, and you will live."

POSTCOLONIAL FEMINIST MISSIOLOGICAL MEANING OF MISSIONARY WOMEN'S STORIES

That's how I narrate the six stories of missionary women. In the end, the narration shows evangelism and missions that provide equal space for women must involve and acknowledge women's testimonies about the Trinitarian God through women's experiences, roles, and understanding of the gospel. Likewise, storytelling as evangelism based on a postcolonial feminist missiological perspective is witnessing the Trinitarian God through the embodied story of the gospel, namely the voices and presence of women who bring hope, liberation, justice, and transformation to the church and society, especially for fellow women.

These six stories or narratives of missionary women were retold based on primary and secondary information obtained from various sources. These sources include, among others, personal writings of female missionaries in letters and annual reports to RMG/UEM, and historical and contemporary publications and literature on missions and evangelism, as well as personal publications or interviews with local female missionaries from Nias.

These six narratives are retold using a postcolonial missiological perspective, which aims to prove the impact of patriarchal culture, which has become an obstacle to the realization of evangelism and missions that provide a fair space for women. This perspective is also useful for analyzing power relations that may be found between Western missionary women and local women in Asia, specifically in Nias, Indonesia. With storytelling, history is written or reinterpreted based on the specific experiences of missionary women who are the producers of the text themselves. Storytelling creates new images of relationships between women in evangelization and restores the meaning of evangelization, which has been distorted by patriarchy and colonialism in the past.

Through the narratives of these missionary women, I find that there are dimensions of the Western civilization paradigm that remain the dominant reference for missionary women. This is because at that time it was this paradigm that dominated mission thinking and practice widely, for example, in the narrative of missionary Hanna Blindow. It is undeniable that Blindow's role, dedication, and thoughts contributed a lot to the development of the Niasan women through education at girls' schools. The Christian presence that Blindow showed while serving in Nias made her a martyr until the end of her life. However, there is an aspect that needs to be criticized, namely Blindow's perspective on local communities that still inherited the idea of domination, namely racism.

Russell's argument about relations formed at the intersection of Christianity and local culture is evident in Blindow's narrative. If Russell sees this encounter in the frame of a conflict between relations of domination and relations of hospitality, then in Blindow's life narrative these two contradictions appear paradoxically. On the one hand, Blindow's meetings with local people, especially Nias women, show a friendly relationship, but at the same time, the impression of dominance exists. This is proven by the continued stigma of Blindow towards local people, especially the local belief that Nias is a "pagan" culture and evil when compared to white people's standards.

Racism, which is formed by the understanding of Western culture as superior, meets the patriarchal character of local Nias culture and also forms a different image when the people of Nias are served by white people. White male missionaries were called *tua*, and white female missionaries were called *gawe*. These two titles for Nias people are given to those who are elders in society in terms of age and level of wisdom. However, this title was never given to nonwhite missionaries and local missionaries who contributed equally to missions and evangelization. This section is a criticism of local people in Nias, who, apart from viewing the West as a sort of parent, are also not free from the residue of racist colonial ways of thinking.

Blindow's change in perspective occurred after she witnessed how God worked for local people. The initial accusations against the Nias girls of being lazy and stubborn finally changed. Blindow admitted that Nias's girls were "like wood growing in the forest." They are persistent, obedient, and loyal to their duties. In the meeting with the Nias people who were seen as the other, Blindow also experienced a transformation. Her view of the people of Nias changed to the positive. This change occurred because of the encounter between Blindow and the Niasan women in everyday life with all its complexity.

Dorothea Richter is known by the people of Nias as a friend who showed hospitality to various communities in Nias. In her ministry, Richter learned to serve diverse communities when she was touched by a Chinese Christian woman who asked, "Why not take care of our little daughters?" Richter's encounter with diverse cultures also transformed her vision of service, which was initially exclusive only to the girls of Nias, into serving a diverse community. Richter encouraged Nias girls to get to know and have connections with other communities, for example, Chinese girls and Batak women's associations in Nias. Richter also realized that in serving the mission institutions in Nias, there was a sense of competition between them and the Catholic nuns who served children in Nias. Richter hoped not to be trapped in competition with fellow women, because they were all sent to work to serve God.

Sonia Parera-Hummel's story is different than others in terms of its background and origins. Parera is an Indonesian woman who married a German missionary and was then sent to be a missionary in Nias. Parera has a hybrid identity that was also in contact with patriarchal culture and traces of colonialism in the mission. Even though Parera came to Nias because of her husband, her service to the people of Nias had a huge impact. The beginning of her service in Nias was with Sunday school children. Over time, Parera's ministry continued to develop into her being a preacher at Sunday services, a lecturer at BNKP Sundermann Seminary, and even a principal at BNKP Hanna Blindow Kindergarten. Apart from that, Parera's ministry also developed among Niasan youth and women, especially female pastors. She was one of the figures who pushed for the representation of female Nias pastors at the BNKP Synod Assembly, which in the past had been represented only by male pastors.

The reproduction of a perspective on mission and evangelization that has a spirit of domination has the effect of repeating mission malpractices in the past, which displaced local religion and culture that might be the source of local community theology. The superior view of missionaries in the practice of evangelization also amputates the missionaries' opportunity to be transformed through encounters with others.

Destalenta Zega, in her encounters with many cultures through the evangelism ministry she carried out, took a more open view. For her, evangelism is not only about giving but also receiving from others. She told a story about mission service in Kyrgyzstan; when she testified about the Lord Jesus to a woman, she also had to learn how to milk a cow. Through her encounters with others, Zega encounters God's hospitality.

Yani Saoiyagö in her service to the local Nias community received more pressure from the very patriarchal side of Nias culture. As one of the first woman pastors at BNKP, Saoiyagö encountered many Niasan men who did not take for granted the ministry of women, especially as leaders in the congregation. Saoiyagö's toughness, wisdom, and endurance in facing the field of service in the culture of Nias society made her an inspirational figure for many other Nias women to become pastors.

This synthesis of six narratives of women missionaries shows aspects of their mission work that illustrate embodied missions that confirm and criticize previous women's mission theories, namely the Christian home, woman's work for woman, world friendship, and partnership. The Christian home theory can be seen in the journey of Sonia Parera-Hummel, who initially accompanied her husband to Nias, but her service grew and she deserved to be recognized as a missionary in Nias. Parera's service also goes beyond the service of a model wife in the domestic sphere because much of her service is in public spaces. Woman's work for woman can be seen in the servants Hanna Blindow and Dorothea Richter, who were initially sent by RMG to serve fellow women in Nias. The beginning of their service was following their mission, but later on, they served not only fellow women. Blindow once served in a congregation, and Richter opened connections with communities outside Nias by embracing the Chinese and Batak communities in Nias. In this way, their service goes beyond the theory of woman's work for woman. Apart from that, their friendship with the Niasan women who are also developing in the service proves the world friendship theory, even though in practice there is still a paternalistic relationship between white women and the local Niasan women. Until now, BNKP is still connected with mission institutions both as members and as partners. Partnership is the theory that describes this relationship.

Evangelism as storytelling based on a postcolonial feminist missiological perspective through six narratives of missionary women shows that the narratives of missionary women must be seen in the frame of an appreciative-critical paradox. First, on the one hand, the presence of missionary women helped encourage individual conversion, and on the other hand, it also encouraged social transformation. Second, on the one hand, the service of women missionaries broke through gender boundaries that previously hampered women's direct involvement in missions and evangelization, but on the other hand, women missionaries were also formed in a patriarchal society with traces of colonial thinking as the characteristics of missions spread widespread at that time. Third, on the one hand, the presence of missionary women transforms the communities they serve, but on the other hand, they also experience a transformation in their thinking, understanding, and relationships with the God they believe in and also with the local community. Two appreciative-critical sides are needed in analyzing the narrative of women missionaries as embodied missions.

CONCLUSION

Women's roles in mission service have long existed. Historical narratives need to appreciate and remember the work and role of women missionaries as part of the history of missions in Nias. Telling the life stories of missionary women is a form of evangelism because, through the journey of their lives, there is testimony of the Trinitarian God. These testimonies are not only witnessed and proclaimed but also embodied in their ministry. By telling women's life stories, women's voices become significant. From a postcolonial feminist perspective, authentic women's voices are appreciated. Women were the first people to witness their own life experiences about the Trinity of God.

At the celebration of Mission Day in Nias, namely every September 27, there is space for worship to read *manö-manö* (stories) about the historical journey of missions in Nias. The figure whose life story is always read about is the first male missionary in Nias, namely Ludwig Ernst Denninger. He was the first RMG missionary envoy on the island of Nias. The celebration of Mission Day in Nias should be a place of appreciation for all those who have been involved in mission work and evangelization, including women missionaries. The life stories of missionary women who testify about God and his work can be read at mission celebrations at BNKP.

Famanö-manö (storytelling) narratives of missionary women is not just a memory of missionary women envoys from the RMG or local Nias missionary women but is a symbol of the voice of liberation and justice for women who have participated in evangelization as a mission. The names of women such as Hanna Blindow, Dorothea Richter, Sonia Parera-Hummel, Masrial Zebua, Destalenta Zega, and Yani Saoiyagö are waiting to be mentioned and remembered by the church as women missionaries.

Bibliography

Adeney, Frances S. "From the Inside Out: Gender Ideologies and Christian Mission in Indonesia." In *Gospel Bearers, Gender Barriers: Missionary Women in the Twentieth Century*, edited by Dana L. Robert, 171–84. American Society of Missiology. New York: Orbis, 2002.

Appelbaum, Steven, et al. "Gender and Leadership? Leadership and Gender? A Journey through the Landscape of Theories." *Leadership and Organization Development Journal* 1 (2003) 43–51.

Bevans, Stephen B., and Roger P. Schroeder. *Constants in Context: Theology of Mission for Today*. American Society of Missiology. Maryknoll, NY: Orbis, 2004.

Blindow, Hannah. "Letter to Rheinische Missionsgesellschaft." [In German.] Multiple dates. In *Frauen und Mädchenarbeit auf Nias: Jahresbericht an Gebetskreise in der Heimat*, archival collection in Vereinte Evangelische Mission [United Evangelical Mission], Wuppertal-Barmen, Germ.

Bosch, David J. *Transforming Mission: Paradigm Shift in Theology of Mission*. American Society of Missiology Series. Maryknoll, NY: Orbis, 1991.

BPHMS BNKP. *Himpunan Hasil Keputusan Persidangan Majelis Sinode Ke-54 Tahun 2007*. BPHMS BNKP: Telukdalam, Indon.: 2007.

BPMS BNKP. *Konfesi Banua Niha Keriso Protestan*. BPHMS BNKP: Gunungsitoli, Indon.: 2021.

———. *Peraturan Banua Niha Keriso Protestan Nomor 12/BPMS-BNKP/2012 Tentang Tertib Penggembalaan*. BPHMS BNKP: Gunungsitoli, Indon.: 2012.

Cantwell, Laurence. "The Gospels as Biographies." *Scottish Journal of Theology* 34 (1981) 193–200. http://journals.cambridge.org/SJT.

Carter, Warren. *Matthew and Empire: Initial Explorations*. New York: Trinity, 2001.

Dube, Musa W. *Postcolonial Feminist Interpretation of the Bible*. St. Louis, MO: Chalice, 2000.

Grau, Marion. *Rethinking Mission in the Postcolony: Salvation, Society and Subversion*. New York: T&T Clark International, 2011.

Gulö, W. *Benih yang Tumbuh XIII: Banua Niha Keriso Protestan*. Salatiga, Indon.: Lembaga Penelitian dan Studi Dewan Gereja-gereja di Indonesia, 1983.

———. *Perjumpaan Injil dan Budaya Nias: Laporan Penelitian*. Jakarta: Panitia Seminar dan Lokakarya Perjumpaan Injil dan Budaya Nias PGI, 2004.

Shital, Gunjate V. "Postcolonial Feminist Theory: An Overview." In *Proceedings of National Seminar on Postmodern Literary Theory and Literature*, 284. Nanded: N.p., 2012.

Harefa, Oinike Natalia. "*Böwö*: A Call to Re-Examine Bride Price." *Feminist Review* 2 (2022) 80–84. https://doi.org/10.1177/01417789221102572.

———. "Perempuan Nias dan Perkawinan: Sebuah Kajian Terhadap Posisi Perempuan Nias dalam Ritus Perkawinan Adat Nias Terkait Mas Kawin, Peranan Perempuan dalam Kehidupan Perkawinan, Serta Pergumulan BNKP dalam Mewujudkan Keadilan bagi Perempuan Nias." BTh thesis, Sekolah Tinggi Teologi Jakarta, 2005.

Hatina, Meir. *Martyrdom in Modern Islam: Piety, Power, and Politics*. New York: Cambridge University Press, 2014.

Hertig, Young Lee. "Without a Face: The Nineteenth-Century Bible Women and Twentieth-Century Female Jeondosa." In *Gospel Bearers, Gender Barriers: Missionary Women in the Twentieth Century*, edited by Dana L. Robert, 185–99. American Society of Missiology. New York: Orbis, 2002.

Heuser, Frederick J., Jr. "*Woman's Work for Woman*, Cultural Change, and the Foreign Missionary Movement." *Journal of Presbyterian History* 75 (1997) 119–30. https://www.jstor.org/stable/23335236.

Hummel, Uwe, and Tuhoni Telaumbanua. *Cross and Adu: A Socio-Historical Study on the Encounter between Christianity and the Indigenous Culture on Nias and Batu Islands, Indonesia (1865–1965)*. Zoetermeer, Neth.: Boekencentrum, 2007.

———. *Salib dan Adu: Studi Sejarah dan Sosial-Budaya Tentang Perjumpaan Kekristenan dan Kebudayaan Asli di Nias dan Pulau-Pulau Batu, Indonesia (1865–1965)*. Jakarta: BPK Gunung Mulia, 2015.

Kennedy, D. James. *Apakah Anda Tahu dengan Pasti?* [Do you know for sure?]. Malang: EE Indonesia, 2012.

———. *Multiplikasi: Evangelism Explosion International Indonesia*. Malang: EE Indonesia, 2012.

Kerr, David A. "Christian Understanding of Proselytism." *International Bulletin of Missionary Research* 23 (1999) 8–12, 14.

Kirk, J. Andrew. *Apa Itu Misi? Suatu Penelusuran Teologis*. Translated by Pericles Katoppo. Jakarta: BPK Gunung Mulia, 2015.

Khoja-Moolji, S., and M. A. Chacko. "Post-Colonialism, Impact on Women." In *The Multimedia Encyclopedia of Women in Today's World*, edited by Mary Z. Stange et al., 1–7. London: Sage, 2011.

Koyama, Kosuke. *Injil dalam Pandangan Asia*. Jakarta: Yayasan Satya Karya, 1976.

Lacugna, Catherine Mowry. "God in Communion with Us: The Trinity." In *Freeing Theology: The Essentials of Theology in Feminist Perspective*, 83–114. New York: HarperCollins, 1993.

Laiya, Bambowo. *Solidaritas Kekeluargaan dalam Salah Satu Masyarakat Desa di Nias—Indonesia*. Yogyakarta: Universitas Gadjah Mada, 1983.

Lakawa, Septemmy E., host. "Menggereja Ekumenis, Misional, Ekologis: Sebuah Perspektif Teologis Biblis Tentang Pekabaran Injil." Panel discussion at Gereja Kristen Oikumene, Jakarta, 2022.

———. "Misiologi Bela Rasa: Misiologi Menurut Seorang Perempuan Kristen Indonesia." MTh thesis, Sekolah Tinggi Teologi Jakarta, 1998.

———. "Misiologi Luka: Mengimajinasikan Ulang Misi di Indonesia Masa Kini." In *Misiologi Kontemporer: Merentangkan Horison Panggilan Kristen*. Jakarta: BPK Gunung Mulia, 2019.

———. "Mission and Evangelism." In *Christianity in East and Southeast Asia*, edited by Kenneth R. Ross et al., 400–412. Edinburgh Companions to Global Christianity. Edinburgh: Edinburgh University Press, 2020.

———. "Risky Hospitality: Mission in the Aftermath of Religious Communal Violence in Indonesia." ThD diss., Boston University, 2011.

Love, John D. "John Henry Newman's *Apologia*: Personal Testimony as a Method of Evangelization and Apologetics." *Newman Studies Journal* 9 (2012) 18–31. https://doi.org/10.1353/nsj.2012.0002.

Majelis Sinode BNKP. *Ketetapan Majelis Sinode BNKP Nomor: II/TAP.MS-BNKP/2007 Tentang Pengesahan dan Penetapan Tata Gereja Banua Niha Keriso Protestan*. Telukdalam, Indon.: Majelis Sinode BNKP, 2007.

McClendon, James Wm., Jr. *Biography as Theology: How Life Stories Can Remake Today's Theology*. New York: Abingdon, 1974.

Meserve, Harry C. "Biography as Theology." *Journal of Religion and Health* 14 (1975) 227–30.

Muck, Terry, and Frances S. Adeney. *Christianity Encountering World Religion: The Practice of Mission in the Twenty-First Century*. Grand Rapids: Baker Academic, 2009.

Neill, Stephen. *Colonialism and Christian Missions*. London: Lutterworth, 1966.

Onyinah, Opoku. "New Ways of Doing Evangelism." *International Review of Mission* 103 (2014) 121–28.

Parveen, Asia. "Feminism: A General Survey." In *Proceedings of National Seminar on Postmodern Literary Theory and Literature*, 344–45. Nanded: N.p., 2012.

PLPI. *Materi Penataran Pelayanan di BNKP: Edisi Khusus Penataran di Resort*. Gunungsitoli, Indon.: PLPI BNKP, 2011.

Pui-lan, Kwok. *Introducing Asian Feminist Theology*. Introductions in Feminist Theology. Sheffield: Sheffield Academic, 2000.

Richter, Dorothea. "Letter to Rheinische Missionsgesellschaft." [In German.] Various dates. In *Frauen und Mädchenarbeit auf Nias: Jahresbericht an Gebetskreise in der Heimat*, archival collection in Vereinte Evangelische Mission [United Evangelical Mission], Wuppertal-Barmen, Germ.

Robert, Dana L. *American Women in Mission: A Social History of Their Thought and Practice*. Macon, GA: Mercer University Press, 1997.

———. *Christian Mission: How Christianity Became a World Religion*. Chichester, Eng.: Wiley-Blackwell, 2009.

———, ed. *Converting Colonialism: Visions and Realities in Mission History, 1706–1914*. Grand Rapids: Eerdmans, 2008.

———. "Cross-Cultural Friendship in the Creation of Twentieth Century World Christianity." *International Bulletin of Missionary Research* 35 (2011) 100–107.

———. "From 'Give Us Friends' to 'Other Sheep I Have': Transnational Friendship and Edinburgh 1910." *ZMiSS* 2–3 (2018) 196–215.

———, ed. *Gospel Bearers, Gender Barriers: Missionary Women in the Twentieth Century*. American Society of Missiology. Maryknoll, NY: Orbis, 2002.

———. "Protestant Women Missionaries: Foreign and Home." In *Encyclopedia of Women and Religion in North America*, edited by Rosemary S. Keller and Rosemary R. Ruether, 2:834–43. Bloomington: Indiana University Press, 2006.

———. "What Happened to the Christian Home? The Missing Component of Mission Theory." *Missiology* 33 (2005) 325–40.

Röhm, Emilie. "Letter to Rheinische Missionsgesellschaft." [In German.] Dec. 31, 1936. In *Frauen und Mädchenarbeit auf Nias: Jahresbericht an Gebetskreise in der Heimat*, archival collection in Vereinte Evangelische Mission [United Evangelical Mission], Wuppertal-Barmen, Germ.

Ruíz, Elena. "Postcolonial and Decolonial Feminism." In *The Oxford Handbook of Feminist Philosophy*, edited by Kim Q. Hall and Ásta, 541–51. Oxford Handbooks. New York: Oxford University Press, 2019.

Russell, Letty M. "Cultural Hermeneutics: A Postcolonial Look at Mission." *Journal of Feminist Studies in Religion* 20 (2004) 23–40.

———. "Encountering the 'Other' in a World of Difference and Danger." *Harvard Theological Review* 99 (2006) 457–68.

Second Vatican Council. "*Ad Gentes*: On the Mission Activity of the Church." Vatican, Dec. 7, 1965. https://www.vatican.va/archive/hist_councils/ii_vatican_council/documents/vat-ii_decree_19651207_ad-gentes_en.html.

Share It. Malang: EE Indonesia, 2020.

Song, Choan-Seng. *Sebutkanlah Nama-Nama Kami: Teologi Cerita dari Perspektif Asia*. Jakarta: BPK Gunung Mulia, 1999.

Spivak, Gayatri Chakravorty. "Can the Subaltern Speak?" In *Reflections on the History of an Idea*, edited by Rosalind C. Morris, 66–111. New York: Columbia University Press, 2010.

———. "Toward a Postcolonial Ethics of Care: In What Interest, to Regulate What Sort of Relationships, Is the Globe Evoked?" Ethics of Care, 2015. https://ethicsofcare.org/wp-content/uploads/2016/12/Toward_a_Postcolonial_Ethics_of_Care.pdf.

Stanley, Brian. *Christianity in the Twentieth Century: A World History*. Princeton, NJ: Princeton University Press, 2018.

Stone, Bryan. *Evangelism after Christendom: The Theology and Practice of Christian Witness*. Grand Rapids: Brazos, 2007.

Suzuki, Peter. *The Religious System and Culture of Nias Indonesia*. The Hague: Excelsior, 1959.

Tanner, Kathryn. *Christ the Key*. Current Issues in Theology 7. Cambridge: Cambridge University Press, 2010.

Tong, Rosemarie Putnam. *Feminist Thought: Pengantar Paling Komprehensif Kepada Arus Utama Pemikiran Feminis*. Yogyakarta: Jalasutra, 2006.

Töpperwien, Annamarie. *Seine "Gehülfin": Wirken und Bewahrung deutscher Missionarsfrauen in Indonesien 1865–1930*. InterCultura: Missions- und kulturgeschichtliche Forschungen 1. Cologne: Köppe, 2004.

WCC. *Together towards Life: Mission and Evangelism in Changing Landscapes*. Geneva: WCC, 2012.

Zebua, Fondrusi. "Letter to Rheinische Missionsgesellschaft." [In German.] Nov. 13, 1953. In *Frauen und Mädchenarbeit auf Nias: Jahresbericht an Gebetskreise in der Heimat*, archival collection in Vereinte Evangelische Mission [United Evangelical Mission], Wuppertal-Barmen, Germ.

Zebua, Masrial. *Sampah menjadi Persembahan: Kisah Transformasi atas Desa yang Dijamah Tuhan*. Jakarta: Yayasan Komunikasi Bina Kasih, 2002.

Zendrato, Taliziduhu. "Okultisme." In *Materi Penataran Pelayan di BNKP: Edisi Khusus Penataran di Resort*, by PLPI, 84–90. Gunungsitoli, Indon.: BNKP, 2011.

www.ingramcontent.com/pod-product-compliance
Lightning Source LLC
Chambersburg PA
CBHW060822190426

43197CB00038B/2199